INTRODUCTION

CHAPTER 1: UNDERSTANDING BLOCKCHAIN FUNDAMENTALS

CHAPTER 2: BLOCKCHAIN'S TRANSFORMATIVE POTENTIAL

CHAPTER 3: LEADERSHIP CHALLENGES AND OPPORTUNITIES

CHAPTER 4: ORGANIZATIONAL TRANSFORMATION

CHAPTER 5: REGULATORY AND LEGAL CONSIDERATIONS

CHAPTER 6: FUTURE OUTLOOK AND RECOMMENDATIONS

CONCLUSION

# Introduction

Blockchain technology is more than just a buzzword; it is a transformative force that is reshaping industries, disrupting traditional business models, and redefining the roles and responsibilities of leaders and managers. The purpose of this book is to serve as a guide for leaders and organizations to understand, adopt, and effectively leverage the power of blockchain technology. By delving deep into its principles, applications, and implications, this book aims to equip readers with the necessary knowledge and strategies to navigate and thrive in a blockchain-driven world.

The first objective of this book is to demystify blockchain technology. Despite its growing popularity, blockchain remains a complex and often misunderstood concept. By breaking down its core principles—decentralization, transparency, and immutability—and explaining key components such as distributed ledgers, consensus mechanisms, and smart contracts, this book will provide a clear and accessible understanding of blockchain technology. This foundational knowledge is essential for leaders who must make informed decisions about integrating blockchain into their organizations.

Beyond the basics, this book will explore the transformative potential of blockchain across various sectors. From finance and supply chain to healthcare and governance, blockchain is enabling new business models, enhancing trust and transparency, and streamlining processes. Through detailed case studies and real-world examples, this book will illustrate how blockchain is being applied in practice, showcasing success stories and highlighting the tangible benefits that organizations can achieve.

Leadership in the blockchain era presents unique challenges and opportunities. Traditional leadership models, which often rely on centralized decision-making and hierarchical structures, may not be well-suited for the decentralized and transparent nature of blockchain. This book will delve into how leadership must evolve to embrace these changes, promoting networked, collaborative, and adaptive leadership styles. It will explore the concept of "leadership on a blockchain" and discuss how leaders can navigate the complexities of decentralized decision-making and distributed authority.

Organizational transformation is another critical theme of this book. Adopting blockchain technology requires more than just technological changes; it necessitates cultural shifts, new governance models, and the integration of blockchain into existing systems and processes. This book will provide strategies for managing this transformation, offering practical advice on fostering a blockchain-friendly organizational culture, managing change, and overcoming resistance.

The regulatory and legal landscape surrounding blockchain is complex and evolving. Compliance, data privacy, and intellectual property rights pose significant challenges for organizations looking to implement blockchain solutions. This book will address these issues, offering guidance on navigating the regulatory environment and ensuring legal compliance.

The book will offer insights into the future of blockchain technology and its potential impact on leadership and organizational structures. It will provide recommendations and best practices for leaders to stay ahead of the curve, foster innovation, and drive their organizations forward in a blockchain-enabled world. This book is designed to be an essential resource for leaders and organizations seeking to understand and harness the power of blockchain technology. By covering a wide range of topics—from foundational concepts to practical applications, leadership challenges to organizational transformation, and regulatory considerations to future outlooks—this book aims to provide a holistic and actionable guide for navigating the blockchain revolution. Whether you are a seasoned executive, a rising leader, or an organizational strategist, this book will equip you with the insights and tools needed to drive meaningful change and achieve success in the blockchain era.

Understanding blockchain technology is crucial for leaders and organizations in the digital age. Blockchain's transformative potential can revolutionize industries by enabling secure, transparent, and decentralized transactions without the need for intermediaries. This fundamental shift can streamline processes, reduce costs, and increase efficiency across various sectors, including finance, supply chain, healthcare, and governance.

Blockchain is not just a technological advancement; it has the potential to revolutionize industries by fundamentally altering how transactions and data sharing occur. By enabling secure, transparent, and decentralized transactions, blockchain removes the need for intermediaries, streamlining processes and reducing costs. In sectors like finance, blockchain can facilitate faster and cheaper transactions. In supply chain management, it can enhance traceability and efficiency. Healthcare can benefit from improved data sharing and security, while governance can become more transparent and accountable.

Blockchain technology enables the creation of new business models and revenue streams. It facilitates peer-to-peer transactions, the tokenization of assets, and the use of smart contracts. These capabilities can lead to innovative business approaches, such as decentralized finance (DeFi), which allows financial transactions without traditional banks, and non-fungible tokens (NFTs), which provide new ways to own and trade digital assets. Understanding blockchain fundamentals is essential for organizations to leverage these opportunities and remain competitive in a rapidly evolving market.

The immutable and distributed nature of blockchain technology promotes unparalleled levels of trust, transparency, and accountability in transactions and data sharing. Every transaction recorded on a blockchain is permanent and visible to all network participants, which reduces the risk of fraud and ensures data integrity. For organizations, understanding how blockchain achieves this transparency can help build stronger relationships with stakeholders, customers, and partners by demonstrating a commitment to openness and accountability.

Blockchain's advanced cryptographic techniques and decentralized architecture significantly enhance data security and privacy. Unlike traditional centralized systems, where a single point of failure can compromise the entire network, blockchain's decentralized nature distributes data across multiple nodes, making it more resilient to attacks. For industries dealing with sensitive information, such as healthcare and finance, comprehending these features is vital. Blockchain can protect patient records, financial transactions, and other critical data from unauthorized access and tampering.

As blockchain adoption grows, so does the need for regulatory frameworks to govern its use. Understanding the technology behind blockchain can help organizations navigate complex compliance requirements and mitigate associated risks. Regulatory bodies worldwide are developing rules to address issues such as data privacy, anti-money laundering (AML), and know-your-customer (KYC) regulations. By staying informed about these developments, organizations can ensure they comply with legal standards while leveraging blockchain's benefits.

Blockchain is poised to be a foundational technology for the next generation of the internet, often referred to as Web3. This future internet landscape will be characterized by decentralized applications and services that offer greater user control and privacy. By gaining knowledge about blockchain now, organizations can position themselves to capitalize on these future opportunities. Understanding blockchain technology enables leaders to develop strategies that incorporate emerging trends, ensuring their organizations stay ahead of the curve and are prepared for the transformative changes blockchain will bring.

Leaders who understand blockchain technology can make informed decisions about its implementation, develop strategies to leverage its benefits, and prepare for the transformative changes it brings. This knowledge allows for a strategic approach to integrating blockchain into business operations, optimizing its potential to drive innovation and efficiency. By comprehensively understanding blockchain, leaders can ensure their organizations are well-positioned to navigate the complexities and harness the opportunities of this revolutionary technology.

Understanding blockchain technology is essential for leaders and organizations to remain competitive, efficient, secure, and future-ready. By embracing blockchain's potential and addressing its challenges, leaders can drive innovation, build trust, and create resilient organizations prepared to thrive in the digital age. This book aims to provide the knowledge and insights necessary for leaders to harness the power of blockchain and lead their organizations into a successful future.

# Chapter 1: Understanding Blockchain Fundamentals

Imagine a world where transactions are recorded not by a central authority, like a bank, but by a network of computers working together in perfect harmony. This is the essence of blockchain technology—a decentralized, distributed digital ledger that securely and permanently records transactions across many computers.

At the heart of blockchain lies the principle of decentralization. Unlike traditional systems that depend on a central authority to manage and validate transactions, blockchain operates through a peer-to-peer network of nodes. Each node in this network has equal authority to validate and record transactions. This collective validation process eliminates the need for a single controlling entity, making the system more resilient and resistant to manipulation. There is no single point of failure; instead, the power is distributed across the entire network.

Transparency is another cornerstone of blockchain technology. Every transaction is visible to all participants within the network, fostering an environment of openness and accountability. This transparency is achieved because the ledger is replicated across multiple nodes, ensuring that everyone has access to the same information. No transaction is hidden; everything is out in the open, promoting trust among participants.

The principle of immutability further enhances the integrity of blockchain. Once a transaction is recorded on the blockchain, it is etched in stone—it cannot be altered or deleted. This permanence is maintained through cryptographic hashing, where each block contains a hash of the previous block, creating an unbreakable chain. If anyone attempts to alter a block, the change would invalidate all subsequent blocks, making tampering virtually impossible.

These core principles—decentralization, transparency, and immutability—combine to make blockchain a secure and trustworthy system for recording and verifying transactions without a central authority. It enables secure peer-to-peer transactions, eliminates the risk of data manipulation, and creates a clear, auditable trail of information. By understanding and leveraging these principles, leaders and organizations can navigate the blockchain revolution, driving innovation and fostering a new era of trust and efficiency in digital transactions.

To fully appreciate the transformative potential of blockchain, it's crucial to understand how it differs from traditional centralized systems. At the core of this distinction is the approach to data management and transaction validation.

In traditional centralized systems, a single entity or authority, such as a bank, government, or corporation, holds the power to manage and validate transactions. This central authority maintains a master ledger, which records all transactions and balances. While this setup can be efficient and straightforward, it also has significant drawbacks. The central authority becomes a single point of failure, meaning that if it is compromised—whether through hacking, technical failures, or corruption—the entire system can be disrupted. Additionally, centralization often requires participants to place a high degree of trust in the authority to act fairly and securely, which can be problematic if the authority is unreliable or malicious.

Blockchain, on the other hand, is inherently decentralized. Instead of a single authority, a network of nodes, each holding a copy of the entire blockchain ledger, collectively validates transactions. This decentralization ensures that no single point of failure exists. If one node fails or is compromised, the integrity of the network remains intact due to the multiple redundant copies of the ledger. Decisions are made through consensus mechanisms, such as Proof of Work or Proof of Stake, which require a majority of nodes to agree on the validity of transactions. This process enhances security and reduces the risk of fraud or manipulation.

Transparency in blockchain systems also sets them apart from traditional centralized systems. In a centralized system, transaction records are typically accessible only to the central authority and select participants. This limited access can lead to a lack of accountability and potential abuses of power. In contrast, blockchain's distributed ledger is openly visible to all participants in the network. This visibility ensures that every transaction is public and verifiable, promoting an unprecedented level of transparency and trust.

Another key difference is the immutability of blockchain records. Traditional centralized systems allow for the modification or deletion of records by the central authority. This capability, while sometimes necessary, can be misused, leading to issues such as fraud or historical revisionism. Blockchain technology, however, employs cryptographic techniques to ensure that once a transaction is added to the blockchain, it cannot be altered or erased. Each block in the chain contains a cryptographic hash of the previous block, forming a secure, unchangeable record. This immutability guarantees a permanent and tamper-proof ledger, which is crucial for maintaining the integrity of transaction histories.

Blockchain also introduces efficiency through automation. Traditional systems often involve numerous intermediaries to verify and process transactions, leading to delays and increased costs. Blockchain eliminates many of these intermediaries by using smart contracts—self-executing contracts with the terms of the agreement directly written into code. These smart contracts automatically execute and enforce the terms when predefined conditions are met, streamlining processes and reducing the potential for human error or fraud.

Data security in blockchain systems benefits from advanced cryptographic techniques and a decentralized architecture. Centralized systems are more vulnerable to data breaches, as they provide hackers with a single target. In contrast, blockchain's distributed nature makes it significantly harder for attackers to compromise the network, as they would need to simultaneously alter the data on the majority of nodes, a task that is nearly impossible given the computational power required.

Blockchain's approach to trust is fundamentally different. Traditional systems often rely on trust in the central authority, which can be problematic if that trust is misplaced or abused. Blockchain builds trust through cryptographic proof and decentralized consensus, reducing the need to rely on potentially fallible or corruptible central authorities. This shift not only enhances security and integrity but also democratizes access and control over data, empowering participants across the network.

The differences between blockchain and traditional centralized systems highlight blockchain's advantages in terms of security, transparency, efficiency, and trust. By decentralizing control, ensuring transparency and immutability, automating processes, and enhancing data security, blockchain technology provides a robust and innovative alternative to traditional centralized approaches. Understanding these differences is essential for leaders and organizations seeking to leverage blockchain's potential and drive transformative change.

It's essential to understand three key concepts: distributed ledgers, consensus mechanisms, and smart contracts. These elements form the backbone of blockchain systems, enabling their decentralized, secure, and efficient operations.

A distributed ledger is a type of database that is replicated, shared, and synchronized across multiple nodes in a network. Unlike a traditional centralized database managed by a single authority, a distributed ledger has no central point of control. Every node in the network maintains an identical copy of the ledger, ensuring that all participants have access to the same information. This decentralization provides several advantages. The ledger is highly resilient to failures or attacks, as its replication across many nodes means that even if several nodes are compromised, the integrity of the ledger remains intact. All transactions recorded on the ledger are visible to all participants, promoting transparency and accountability. Additionally, the distributed nature of the ledger makes it difficult for malicious actors to alter transaction records. Any attempt to tamper with a single copy of the ledger would be quickly identified and rejected by the other nodes.

Consensus mechanisms are protocols that ensure all nodes in a blockchain network agree on the validity of transactions and the state of the ledger. These mechanisms are crucial for maintaining the integrity and security of the blockchain. There are several types of consensus mechanisms, but two of the most widely used are Proof of Work (Pow) and Proof of Stake (PoS). In PoW, nodes, known as miners, compete to solve complex mathematical puzzles. The first node to solve the puzzle gets to add the next block of transactions to the blockchain and is rewarded with cryptocurrency. This process requires significant computational power, making it expensive and time-consuming, but it ensures that adding new blocks is a secure and deliberate process. In contrast, PoS selects the creator of a new block based on the number of tokens they hold and are willing to "stake" as collateral. This approach is more energy-efficient than PoW, as it does not require extensive computational resources. PoS encourages network participants to act in the network's best interest, as their stake is at risk if they attempt to validate fraudulent transactions. Other consensus mechanisms include Delegated Proof of Stake (DPoS), Practical Byzantine Fault Tolerance (PBFT), and many more, each with its own strengths and use cases.

Smart contracts are self-executing contracts with the terms of the agreement directly written into code. These contracts automatically enforce and execute the terms when predefined conditions are met, eliminating the need for intermediaries and reducing the potential for disputes. Key features of smart contracts include automation, accuracy, security, and trust. Smart contracts automatically execute transactions once the conditions are satisfied, streamlining processes and reducing the need for manual intervention. The code specifies the exact terms and conditions, reducing the risk of misunderstandings or errors. Smart contracts are stored on the blockchain, inheriting its security and immutability. Once deployed, they cannot be altered, ensuring that the agreed-upon terms are always enforced. Parties can trust that the contract will be executed as programmed, without the need for intermediaries or enforcement agencies. For example, in a supply chain scenario, a smart contract could automatically release payment to a supplier once goods are delivered and verified. This reduces delays and ensures that all parties adhere to the agreed terms without manual oversight.

By integrating distributed ledgers, consensus mechanisms, and smart contracts, blockchain technology creates a robust, secure, and transparent system for recording and verifying transactions. These key concepts enable blockchain to revolutionize traditional systems, offering new opportunities for innovation and efficiency. Understanding these foundational elements is crucial for leaders and organizations aiming to harness the full potential of blockchain technology. This comprehensive understanding will empower leaders to make informed decisions about blockchain implementation, develop strategies to leverage its benefits, and prepare their organizations for the transformative changes that blockchain brings across various sectors.

To navigate the blockchain revolution effectively, understanding its underlying technology is crucial for effective leadership. Leaders who grasp the intricacies of blockchain can make informed decisions, leverage its potential benefits, and steer their organizations through the complexities of this transformative technology.

A solid understanding of blockchain technology enables leaders to identify and seize new opportunities. By comprehending how distributed ledgers, consensus mechanisms, and smart contracts work, leaders can envision innovative applications that drive efficiency, transparency, and cost savings. This knowledge allows them to strategically integrate blockchain into their business models, creating competitive advantages and opening up new revenue streams.

Understanding blockchain is vital for managing organizational change. Adopting blockchain technology often requires significant shifts in processes, culture, and even organizational structures. Leaders equipped with blockchain knowledge can effectively communicate its benefits to their teams, address concerns, and foster a culture of innovation and adaptability. They can guide their organizations through the transition, ensuring that employees are well-informed and prepared to embrace new ways of working.

Effective leadership in the blockchain era also involves navigating regulatory and legal landscapes. Blockchain's decentralized nature and the advent of smart contracts introduce new compliance challenges. Leaders who understand these complexities can better anticipate regulatory changes, ensure compliance, and mitigate risks. This proactive approach not only protects the organization but also positions it as a responsible and forward-thinking player in the industry.

Blockchain technology enhances data security and privacy, critical concerns for any organization. Leaders who understand blockchain's cryptographic foundations can implement robust security measures, protecting sensitive information and maintaining stakeholder trust. This expertise is particularly valuable in industries such as finance, healthcare, and supply chain management, where data integrity and security are paramount.

In addition to these practical benefits, understanding blockchain technology fosters visionary leadership. Leaders who are well-versed in blockchain can foresee its broader implications for their industry and society. They can contribute to shaping the future of technology, influencing industry standards, and participating in global conversations about the ethical and social impacts of blockchain. This thought leadership not only enhances their organization's reputation but also ensures it remains at the forefront of technological innovation.

A deep understanding of blockchain technology is essential for effective leadership in today's digital age. It empowers leaders to innovate, manage change, navigate regulatory environments, enhance data security, and provide visionary guidance. As blockchain continues to evolve and reshape industries, leaders who invest in understanding this technology will be better equipped to lead their organizations to success in a decentralized future. By mastering blockchain, leaders can drive transformation, build trust, and position their organizations for long-term success. This foundational knowledge sets the stage for exploring blockchain's transformative potential in various sectors, which we will delve into in the next chapter.

# Chapter 2: Blockchain's Transformative Potential

Blockchain technology is revolutionizing industries by enabling secure, transparent, and decentralized transactions. This chapter explores the profound impact of blockchain across various sectors, starting with finance, and highlights how its core principles are driving innovation and efficiency.

The financial sector has been one of the earliest and most significant adopters of blockchain technology. Blockchain's ability to provide secure, transparent, and immutable transaction records addresses many challenges in the financial industry, such as fraud, inefficiency, and lack of transparency.

One of the primary applications of blockchain in finance is in the realm of payments and remittances. Traditional cross-border payments can be slow, costly, and complex, often involving multiple intermediaries. Blockchain streamlines this process by enabling peer-to-peer transactions that are faster, cheaper, and more secure. For example, Ripple's blockchain-based payment protocol allows for instant, low-cost international money transfers, reducing the need for intermediary banks and improving transaction speed.

Blockchain also plays a crucial role in enhancing the transparency and efficiency of securities trading. Traditional securities settlement processes can take several days to finalize, creating risks and inefficiencies. Blockchain can automate and expedite the settlement process through smart contracts, which execute and enforce the terms of agreements automatically. This not only reduces settlement times but also minimizes the risk of errors and fraud. Projects like the Australian Securities Exchange (ASX) are exploring blockchain to replace their current clearing and settlement system, aiming for greater efficiency and lower costs.

In the realm of fundraising and investment, blockchain has given rise to new methods such as Initial Coin Offerings (ICOs) and Security Token Offerings (STOs). These fundraising mechanisms allow companies to raise capital by issuing digital tokens on a blockchain, which can represent various assets or rights. This democratizes access to investment opportunities, enabling a broader range of investors to participate and providing startups with an alternative to traditional venture capital.

Blockchain's ability to provide an immutable and transparent ledger makes it ideal for supply chain management. Traditional supply chains are often complex, involving numerous parties and a lack of visibility, which can lead to inefficiencies and increased risk of fraud. Blockchain addresses these issues by providing a single, transparent source of truth for all transactions and movements of goods.

For instance, blockchain can track the provenance of goods, ensuring that products are sourced ethically and sustainably. Companies like IBM and Walmart have implemented blockchain solutions to trace the journey of food products from farm to table, improving food safety and enabling rapid responses to contamination incidents. This traceability not only enhances consumer trust but also helps companies comply with regulatory requirements.

Smart contracts can further streamline supply chain operations by automating various processes, such as payments and inventory management. For example, a smart contract can automatically trigger a payment to a supplier once goods are delivered and verified, reducing delays and ensuring timely transactions. This automation reduces the reliance on intermediaries and minimizes the risk of disputes.

In the healthcare sector, blockchain technology addresses critical issues related to data security, interoperability, and patient privacy. The decentralized nature of blockchain ensures that patient records are secure and tamper-proof, mitigating the risk of data breaches and unauthorized access.

Blockchain facilitates secure sharing of medical records among healthcare providers, improving coordination and care quality. Patients can grant access to their medical history through blockchain, ensuring that healthcare professionals have accurate and up-to-date information. This interoperability reduces redundant tests and procedures, leading to cost savings and better patient outcomes.

Blockchain can enhance the integrity of pharmaceutical supply chains. By tracking the journey of drugs from manufacturer to consumer, blockchain helps prevent counterfeit medications from entering the market. Companies like Chronicled are leveraging blockchain to ensure the authenticity and safety of pharmaceuticals, thereby protecting public health. Blockchain's transparency and immutability offer significant benefits for governance and public administration. Governments can use blockchain to enhance transparency, reduce corruption, and improve the efficiency of public services.

One notable application is in the area of voting systems. Blockchain-based voting platforms provide a secure and transparent way to conduct elections, ensuring that votes are accurately recorded and cannot be tampered with. This can increase voter trust and participation, as well as reduce the costs and complexities associated with traditional voting methods. Countries like Estonia are pioneering blockchain-based e-voting systems to enhance their electoral processes.

Blockchain can also streamline the management of public records, such as property titles, identity documents, and licenses. By digitizing and securing these records on a blockchain, governments can reduce fraud, improve accessibility, and enhance administrative efficiency. For example, the government of Georgia has implemented a blockchain-based land registry system to provide transparent and immutable records of property ownership. This technology is driving significant transformations across various sectors. In finance, it enhances transaction speed, security, and transparency. In supply chain management, it improves traceability and efficiency. In healthcare, it secures patient data and enhances interoperability. In governance, it promotes transparency and reduces corruption. As blockchain technology continues to evolve, its impact on these and other sectors will likely expand, offering new opportunities for innovation and growth. This comprehensive understanding of blockchain's transformative potential sets the stage for exploring the unique leadership challenges and opportunities presented by this revolutionary technology, which will be discussed in the next chapter.

This technology is profoundly transforming the financial sector, addressing longstanding challenges and opening up new opportunities. By providing secure, transparent, and immutable transaction records, blockchain is revolutionizing how financial transactions are conducted, enhancing efficiency, reducing costs, and fostering innovation.

One of the most significant impacts of blockchain in finance is in the realm of payments and remittances. Traditional cross-border payments are often slow, expensive, and complicated due to the involvement of multiple intermediaries, such as correspondent banks. Blockchain streamlines this process by enabling peer-to-peer transactions, which are faster, cheaper, and more secure.

For instance, Ripple's blockchain-based payment protocol allows for instant, low-cost international money transfers by connecting banks directly through its decentralized network. This eliminates the need for intermediary banks, reducing transaction fees and processing times significantly. Similarly, Stellar provides a platform for low-cost, efficient remittances, making financial services more accessible, especially in underserved regions.

Blockchain technology is also transforming securities trading by enhancing transparency, reducing settlement times, and minimizing risks. In traditional systems, the settlement of securities transactions can take several days, during which time counterparty risk is present, and funds are tied up. Blockchain can automate and expedite the settlement process through smart contracts, which execute and enforce the terms of agreements automatically and in real-time.

Projects like the Australian Securities Exchange (ASX) are exploring the use of blockchain to replace their current clearing and settlement system. By implementing a blockchain-based solution, ASX aims to reduce settlement times from days to mere minutes, increase operational efficiency, and lower costs. This innovation not only benefits the financial institutions involved but also enhances the overall stability and efficiency of financial markets.

Blockchain has introduced new methods of fundraising and investment through Initial Coin Offerings (ICOs) and Security Token Offerings (STOs). These mechanisms allow companies to raise capital by issuing digital tokens on a blockchain, which can represent various assets or rights.

ICOs enable startups to bypass traditional venture capital routes by selling tokens directly to investors, democratizing access to investment opportunities. However, the regulatory landscape for ICOs is evolving to address concerns about fraud and investor protection. In response, STOs have emerged as a compliant alternative, offering tokens that are subject to securities regulations and providing greater investor security.

By leveraging blockchain for fundraising, companies can access a broader pool of investors, streamline the fundraising process, and potentially raise capital more quickly and efficiently than through traditional means.

Blockchain's immutable and transparent nature significantly strengthens fraud prevention and security within the financial sector. Traditional financial systems are vulnerable to fraud, as transactions can be manipulated or falsified by malicious actors. Blockchain's decentralized ledger ensures that once a transaction is recorded, it cannot be altered or deleted. This immutability provides a reliable and tamper-proof record of all transactions. Blockchain employs advanced cryptographic techniques to secure data, making it highly resistant to hacking and fraud. Financial institutions can use blockchain to verify the authenticity of transactions, detect fraudulent activities in real-time, and enhance overall security measures.

Blockchain technology also plays a critical role in improving regulatory compliance and risk management. Financial institutions face stringent regulatory requirements, including Anti-Money Laundering (AML) and Know Your Customer (KYC) regulations. Blockchain can streamline compliance processes by providing a transparent and auditable record of all transactions, making it easier for institutions to demonstrate compliance to regulators. It can facilitate the secure and efficient sharing of KYC data among financial institutions. Instead of each institution conducting its own KYC checks, a verified KYC record can be stored on the blockchain and accessed by multiple institutions, reducing redundancy, costs, and compliance risks.

One of the most groundbreaking applications of blockchain in finance is the emergence of Decentralized Finance (DeFi). DeFi refers to a system of financial applications built on blockchain networks that operate without traditional intermediaries like banks or brokers. DeFi platforms offer a wide range of financial services, including lending, borrowing, trading, and investing, all facilitated by smart contracts.

DeFi platforms like MakerDAO, Aave, and Uniswap have gained significant traction, enabling users to access financial services in a decentralized manner. For example, MakerDAO allows users to lock cryptocurrency as collateral and issue a stablecoin, DAI, against it. Aave facilitates decentralized lending and borrowing, while Uniswap provides a decentralized exchange for trading cryptocurrencies.

The DeFi ecosystem is rapidly growing, offering innovative financial products and services that are accessible to anyone with an internet connection. This democratization of finance has the potential to increase financial inclusion, particularly in regions with limited access to traditional banking services.

Blockchain's transparent nature enhances transparency and accountability within the financial sector. By recording all transactions on a public ledger, blockchain ensures that financial activities are visible and verifiable by all network participants. This transparency reduces the potential for fraudulent activities and promotes trust among stakeholders.

For example, blockchain can provide transparent tracking of charitable donations, ensuring that funds are used as intended and increasing donor confidence. In capital markets, blockchain can improve the transparency of shareholder voting and corporate governance, enhancing accountability and trust between companies and their investors.

Blockchain technology is revolutionizing the financial sector by enhancing efficiency, reducing costs, and fostering innovation. Its applications in payments and remittances, securities trading, fundraising, fraud prevention, regulatory compliance, and decentralized finance are transforming traditional financial systems and creating new opportunities for growth and inclusion. As blockchain continues to evolve, its impact on finance will likely expand, driving further innovation and reshaping the future of the financial industry. This understanding of blockchain's transformative potential sets the stage for exploring its impact on other sectors, which we will delve into in the following sections.

Blockchain technology is profoundly transforming supply chain management by enhancing transparency, traceability, efficiency, and trust. These improvements address many of the longstanding challenges in traditional supply chains, such as lack of visibility, inefficiencies, and vulnerability to fraud. Here's how blockchain is revolutionizing supply chain management:

One of the most significant impacts of blockchain in supply chains is its ability to provide an immutable and transparent ledger that records every transaction and movement of goods. Traditional supply chains often involve multiple parties, with each maintaining its own records. This fragmentation can lead to discrepancies, inefficiencies, and difficulties in tracking the provenance of goods.

Blockchain solves this by creating a single, decentralized record of all transactions that is visible to all participants. For example, when a product moves from a manufacturer to a distributor, then to a retailer, each transaction is recorded on the blockchain. This transparency ensures that all stakeholders have access to the same information, reducing the risk of disputes and enabling quick resolution when issues arise.

In the food industry, blockchain is being used to trace the journey of food products from farm to table. Companies like IBM and Walmart have implemented blockchain solutions to track food items, ensuring that consumers receive safe and authentic products. If a contamination issue arises, blockchain allows for rapid identification of the affected products and their sources, facilitating swift recalls and minimizing harm. Blockchain can significantly streamline supply chain operations by eliminating intermediaries and automating processes. Traditional supply chains often involve numerous intermediaries, each adding their own markup and processing time, which increases costs and delays.

Smart contracts on the blockchain automate various supply chain processes, such as payments and inventory management. For instance, a smart contract can automatically release payment to a supplier once the delivery of goods is confirmed. This reduces the need for manual intervention, speeds up transactions, and ensures that payments are made promptly.

In addition to automating payments, blockchain can also enhance inventory management by providing real-time visibility into stock levels. This allows companies to better manage their inventory, reduce waste, and optimize their supply chain operations.

Blockchain's immutable ledger helps prevent fraud and counterfeiting in supply chains. By providing a verifiable record of a product's journey, blockchain ensures that the authenticity of goods can be easily verified at each stage of the supply chain.

This is particularly valuable in industries where counterfeiting is a major concern, such as pharmaceuticals, luxury goods, and electronics. For example, in the pharmaceutical industry, blockchain can track the production and distribution of drugs, ensuring that only genuine products reach consumers. Companies like Chronicled are using blockchain to verify the authenticity of pharmaceuticals, reducing the risk of counterfeit drugs entering the market.

In the luxury goods sector, blockchain can be used to authenticate products like designer handbags, watches, and jewelry. Each item can be assigned a unique digital identity on the blockchain, which records its entire history, from production to sale. This provides consumers with confidence that they are purchasing genuine items and helps brands protect their reputation.

Blockchain also facilitates compliance with regulatory requirements and promotes sustainable practices in supply chains. Regulations often require detailed documentation of a product's journey, including its origin, handling, and environmental impact. Blockchain provides a transparent and immutable record of this information, making it easier for companies to demonstrate compliance.

In terms of sustainability, blockchain can help track and verify the environmental impact of products. For instance, consumers and regulators can verify that a product was sourced ethically and sustainably. Companies can use blockchain to provide proof of sustainable practices, such as fair labor conditions and environmentally friendly production methods. This transparency can enhance brand reputation and meet the growing consumer demand for ethically produced goods.

Blockchain technology fosters collaboration among supply chain participants by providing a shared, trusted ledger. In traditional supply chains, trust is often a major issue, as participants may be reluctant to share information or collaborate fully due to concerns about data integrity and competitive advantage.

By providing a secure and transparent platform for sharing information, blockchain enhances trust among supply chain partners. This collaborative approach can lead to more efficient and resilient supply chains, as participants are more willing to share data and work together to solve common challenges.

For example, in the automotive industry, manufacturers, suppliers, and logistics providers can use blockchain to share real-time information about parts and components. This improves coordination, reduces delays, and ensures that production schedules are met.

Numerous companies across various industries are already leveraging blockchain to transform their supply chains. For example, Maersk, the global shipping giant, has partnered with IBM to create TradeLens, a blockchain-based platform that digitizes the entire shipping process. TradeLens provides end-to-end visibility of shipments, streamlines documentation, and enhances security, resulting in more efficient and reliable global trade.

Another example is Provenance, a UK-based startup that uses blockchain to track the origins and journeys of products in the food and beverage industry. Provenance's platform allows consumers to verify the authenticity and sustainability of the products they purchase, enhancing transparency and trust.

Blockchain technology is revolutionizing supply chain management by enhancing transparency, traceability, efficiency, and trust. Its applications in improving authenticity, reducing fraud, ensuring compliance, and fostering collaboration are transforming traditional supply chains and creating new opportunities for innovation and growth. As blockchain continues to evolve, its impact on supply chains will likely expand, driving further efficiencies and reshaping the future of global trade. This understanding of blockchain's transformative potential in supply chain management sets the stage for exploring its impact on other critical sectors, such as healthcare and governance, which we will delve into in the following sections. Blockchain technology is revolutionizing the healthcare sector by enhancing data security, improving interoperability, ensuring patient privacy, and streamlining processes. These improvements address many of the critical challenges faced by the healthcare industry, such as fragmented data, inefficiencies, and the need for more robust data protection. Here's how blockchain is transforming healthcare:

Healthcare organizations handle vast amounts of sensitive patient information, making data security a paramount concern. Traditional centralized systems are vulnerable to breaches, which can result in the unauthorized access and misuse of personal health data. Blockchain's decentralized architecture and advanced cryptographic techniques significantly enhance data security by providing a tamper-proof and transparent way to store and manage patient records.

Blockchain ensures that once patient data is recorded, it cannot be altered or deleted without consensus from the network. This immutability protects against data tampering and fraud. Furthermore, because data is distributed across multiple nodes, there is no single point of failure, making it more resistant to attacks. This increased security fosters greater trust among patients and healthcare providers.

One of the significant challenges in healthcare is the lack of interoperability between different systems and providers. Patient data is often scattered across various databases, making it difficult for healthcare providers to access a complete and accurate medical history. This fragmentation can lead to redundant tests, misdiagnoses, and suboptimal patient care.

Blockchain can solve this problem by creating a unified, decentralized ledger of patient data that is accessible to all authorized parties. Through blockchain, patients can control their health information and grant access to different providers as needed. This ensures that healthcare professionals have a comprehensive view of a patient's medical history, leading to better-informed decisions and improved care coordination.

For example, a patient visiting a new doctor can share their complete medical history stored on a blockchain, including past treatments, medications, and test results. This seamless sharing of information reduces the need for repetitive tests and speeds up the diagnostic process.

Patient privacy is a critical concern in healthcare, with strict regulations such as the Health Insurance Portability and Accountability Act (HIPAA) in the United States mandating the protection of personal health information. Blockchain technology enhances patient privacy by allowing individuals to control their data.

Using blockchain, patients can manage who has access to their health information and for how long. They can grant and revoke access permissions in real-time, ensuring that their data is only shared with trusted parties. This decentralized control over personal health information aligns with regulatory requirements and gives patients greater confidence in how their data is handled. Blockchain's transparency allows patients to see a clear audit trail of who accessed their data and when. This transparency increases accountability and helps ensure that privacy practices are followed.

Blockchain can also streamline clinical trials and medical research by providing a transparent and immutable record of all trial data. This includes patient recruitment, consent forms, trial protocols, and results. By recording each step on the blockchain, researchers can ensure the integrity of the data and enhance trust in the results. For example, the blockchain can be used to verify patient consent and participation in a trial, ensuring that ethical standards are met. Researchers can track and validate each phase of the trial, reducing the risk of data manipulation and improving the reproducibility of results.

Blockchain can also facilitate data sharing among researchers, promoting collaboration and accelerating the pace of medical advancements. Researchers can securely share data with colleagues around the world, knowing that the blockchain ensures the accuracy and security of the information.

The pharmaceutical supply chain is complex and often vulnerable to the infiltration of counterfeit drugs, which pose serious risks to patient safety. Blockchain technology can enhance the traceability of pharmaceutical products from manufacture to delivery, ensuring that only authentic medications reach consumers.

By recording every transaction in the drug supply chain on a blockchain, stakeholders can verify the origin and journey of each product. This transparency helps detect and eliminate counterfeit drugs, ensuring that patients receive safe and effective medications. Companies like Chronicled and IBM are already leveraging blockchain to improve the integrity of the pharmaceutical supply chain.

A blockchain-based system can track a drug from the manufacturing plant through the distribution network to the pharmacy, providing a transparent and immutable record of its journey. This traceability makes it much harder for counterfeit drugs to enter the supply chain.

Blockchain can streamline billing and claims processes in healthcare by providing a transparent and automated way to handle transactions. Traditional billing systems are often plagued by inefficiencies, errors, and fraud. Blockchain's smart contracts can automate billing and claims processing, reducing administrative overhead and minimizing the potential for fraud. For example, a smart contract can automatically process insurance claims once predefined conditions are met, such as the completion of a medical procedure. This automation reduces the time and effort required for manual processing and ensures that payments are made promptly and accurately.

In addition, blockchain's transparency allows patients, providers, and insurers to verify billing and claims information easily. This reduces disputes and enhances trust among all parties involved.

Several organizations and initiatives are already utilizing blockchain to transform healthcare. For instance, MedRec, developed by MIT, uses blockchain to create a decentralized record-keeping system that allows patients to manage access to their health information. MedRec aims to improve data sharing among healthcare providers while giving patients control over their medical records.

Another example is SimplyVital Health, which leverages blockchain to enhance care coordination and data management in value-based care models. Their Health Nexus platform uses blockchain to provide a secure, transparent way to share and manage patient data, improving outcomes and reducing costs.

Blockchain technology is revolutionizing healthcare by enhancing data security, improving interoperability, ensuring patient privacy, streamlining clinical trials and research, combating counterfeit drugs, and optimizing billing and claims processes. Its applications are addressing many of the critical challenges faced by the healthcare industry, leading to more efficient, secure, and patient-centered care. As blockchain continues to evolve, its impact on healthcare will likely expand, driving further innovations and improvements in health services. This understanding of blockchain's transformative potential in healthcare sets the stage for exploring its impact on other critical sectors, such as governance and public administration, which we will delve into in the following sections.

This technology is set to revolutionize government and governance by enhancing transparency, reducing corruption, improving efficiency, and fostering greater trust between citizens and public institutions. Its decentralized and immutable nature provides a robust framework for various applications that can significantly transform how governments operate and deliver services.

One of the most profound impacts of blockchain on government is its ability to enhance transparency and accountability. Traditional government systems often suffer from opacity, where decisions and transactions are not always visible to the public. This lack of transparency can lead to corruption and erode public trust.

Blockchain can address these issues by creating a transparent and immutable record of government transactions and decisions. For instance, public expenditures can be recorded on a blockchain, allowing citizens to see exactly how tax revenues are being spent. This transparency can help ensure that funds are used appropriately and reduce opportunities for corruption. Blockchain can be used to track the progress of government projects, providing real-time updates and immutable records of milestones and expenditures. This level of transparency not only holds public officials accountable but also builds trust with citizens by demonstrating that the government is operating with integrity and efficiency.

Blockchain technology can streamline various public services, making them more efficient and accessible. Government processes often involve multiple layers of bureaucracy, which can lead to delays, inefficiencies, and high costs. Blockchain's ability to automate and secure transactions can significantly reduce these inefficiencies. For example, blockchain can simplify the process of issuing and verifying government documents such as birth certificates, marriage licenses, and passports. Instead of relying on paper records and manual verification processes, these documents can be securely stored and verified on a blockchain. This not only speeds up the issuance process but also reduces the risk of fraud and errors.

In Estonia, a pioneer in digital governance, blockchain is used to secure the national health, judicial, legislative, security, and commercial code systems. Citizens can access a wide range of e-government services online, from voting to signing documents, all secured by blockchain technology. This digital transformation has made public services more efficient, transparent, and user-friendly.

Voting systems are another area where blockchain can have a significant impact. Traditional voting methods are often plagued by issues such as voter fraud, low turnout, and lack of transparency. Blockchain-based voting systems can address these challenges by providing a secure, transparent, and tamper-proof way to conduct elections.

With blockchain, each vote is recorded as a transaction on an immutable ledger, ensuring that votes cannot be altered or deleted. This enhances the integrity of the voting process and increases public trust in election outcomes. Additionally, blockchain can enable remote and online voting, making it more convenient for citizens to participate in elections and potentially increasing voter turnout.

Countries like Estonia and Switzerland have already experimented with blockchain-based voting systems. These systems allow for secure and transparent elections, where citizens can verify that their votes have been counted correctly. This not only improves the democratic process but also builds confidence in the electoral system.

Blockchain technology can revolutionize identity management by providing secure and verifiable digital identities. Traditional identity management systems often rely on physical documents and centralized databases, which can be vulnerable to fraud, theft, and unauthorized access. This technology can create decentralized and tamper-proof digital identities that individuals control. These digital identities can be used for a wide range of applications, from accessing government services to verifying personal information online. By storing identity data on a blockchain, individuals can control who has access to their information and ensure that it is secure and accurate.

In India, the government is exploring the use of blockchain to enhance the Aadhaar system, a unique identification system for residents. Blockchain can help secure the identity data, prevent unauthorized access, and ensure that the information is accurate and up-to-date. This can improve the delivery of government services and reduce the risk of identity fraud.

Land and property registries are critical for establishing ownership and facilitating transactions. Traditional systems often involve complex paperwork, lengthy processes, and risks of fraud and disputes. Blockchain can simplify and secure these processes by providing an immutable and transparent record of property ownership and transactions.

By recording property transactions on a blockchain, governments can ensure that ownership records are accurate, tamper-proof, and easily verifiable. This can reduce disputes over property ownership, speed up transactions, and increase trust in the system. Countries like Georgia and Sweden have implemented blockchain-based land registry systems to enhance the efficiency and security of property transactions.

In Georgia, the National Agency of Public Registry uses blockchain to record property transactions, ensuring that records are secure and transparent. This has reduced the time and cost associated with property transfers and increased trust in the land registry system.

Blockchain's transparency and immutability make it a powerful tool in the fight against corruption. By recording all government transactions on a public ledger, blockchain makes it difficult for corrupt officials to hide illicit activities. This transparency can act as a deterrent to corruption and increase accountability. For example, blockchain can be used to track government procurement processes, ensuring that contracts are awarded fairly and transparently. All bids and transactions can be recorded on the blockchain, providing an immutable record that can be audited by the public. This can reduce opportunities for bribery and favoritism, ensuring that government resources are used efficiently and ethically.

Several governments and organizations are already leveraging blockchain to improve governance and public administration. For instance, the government of Dubai aims to become the first blockchain-powered government by 2020. The Dubai Blockchain Strategy includes over 20 blockchain projects in various sectors, including finance, health, transportation, and urban planning. These projects aim to enhance government efficiency, reduce costs, and improve public services. Another example is the United Nations, which has explored the use of blockchain to improve the delivery of humanitarian aid. By using blockchain to track the distribution of aid and verify the identity of recipients, the UN can ensure that resources reach those who need them most and reduce fraud and mismanagement.

Blockchain technology is transforming government and governance by enhancing transparency, reducing corruption, improving efficiency, and fostering greater trust between citizens and public institutions. Its applications in secure identity management, streamlined public services, transparent voting systems, and anti-corruption efforts are revolutionizing traditional governance models and creating new opportunities for innovation and growth. As blockchain continues to evolve, its impact on government and governance will likely expand, driving further improvements and reshaping the future of public administration. This comprehensive understanding of blockchain's transformative potential sets the stage for exploring the unique leadership challenges and opportunities presented by this revolutionary technology, which will be discussed in the next chapter.

# Chapter 3: Leadership Challenges and Opportunities

As blockchain technology continues to disrupt various industries, traditional leadership models must evolve to adapt to this new paradigm. The decentralized, transparent, and immutable nature of blockchain presents unique challenges and opportunities for leaders, requiring a shift from conventional hierarchical structures to more networked, collaborative, and adaptive approaches.

One of the most significant changes introduced by blockchain is the shift towards decentralized decision-making. In traditional organizations, decision-making authority is typically concentrated at the top of the hierarchy. Leaders make decisions that are then passed down through the organizational structure. This model can be effective in stable environments but often struggles to adapt quickly to change and innovation.

Blockchain, with its decentralized architecture, distributes decision-making authority across a network of participants. This requires leaders to embrace a more collaborative approach, where decisions are made through consensus rather than top-down directives. For example, in a blockchain-based organization or Decentralized Autonomous Organization (DAO), decisions about project funding or strategic direction are often made by token holders who vote on proposals. This model promotes inclusivity and ensures that a diverse range of perspectives are considered.

Leaders in this new environment must learn to facilitate and guide consensus-building processes, fostering an inclusive culture where all voices are heard and valued. This requires strong communication skills, the ability to manage diverse stakeholder interests, and a commitment to transparency and fairness.

Blockchain's inherent transparency transforms how leaders manage accountability within their organizations. Traditional leadership often involves a degree of opacity, with information flowing through established channels and potentially being withheld or selectively shared. This can lead to issues of mistrust and lack of accountability.

With blockchain, all transactions and decisions are recorded on an immutable ledger that is visible to all network participants. This level of transparency ensures that actions are open to scrutiny, promoting accountability and ethical conduct. Leaders can no longer rely on opaque practices and must instead operate in a way that withstands public and stakeholder scrutiny.

To thrive in this transparent environment, leaders must embrace open communication and demonstrate integrity in their actions. Building a culture of trust becomes paramount, as does the ability to clearly articulate the rationale behind decisions. Leaders must also be prepared to accept feedback and make adjustments based on collective input, fostering an environment of continuous improvement and shared accountability.

The rapid pace of technological change and the complex nature of blockchain ecosystems require leaders to adopt adaptive and networked leadership styles. Unlike traditional command-and-control models, adaptive leadership involves being flexible and responsive to changing circumstances. This means leaders must be comfortable with uncertainty and able to pivot strategies quickly in response to new information or emerging trends.

Networked leadership emphasizes the importance of relationships and collaboration across organizational boundaries. In a blockchain environment, value is often created through partnerships and alliances with other organizations, developers, and communities. Leaders must therefore be skilled at building and maintaining these networks, leveraging collective expertise, and fostering a sense of shared purpose.

For example, a leader in a blockchain startup might collaborate with external developers to co-create a new decentralized application (dApp). This requires not only technical understanding but also the ability to coordinate efforts, manage diverse contributions, and align everyone towards a common goal.

Blockchain technology drives innovation by enabling new business models, products, and services. Leaders must cultivate a culture that encourages experimentation and creativity while managing the risks associated with innovative ventures. This involves creating an environment where team members feel safe to propose bold ideas and take calculated risks.

To foster such a culture, leaders should prioritize continuous learning and development. This means investing in education and training to keep the team updated on the latest blockchain advancements and industry trends. Encouraging cross-functional collaboration can also spark innovation by bringing together diverse perspectives and skill sets. Furthermore, leaders must be adept at identifying and nurturing talent within their organizations. This involves recognizing and rewarding innovative thinking and ensuring that employees have the resources and support needed to bring their ideas to fruition. By championing innovation and celebrating successes, leaders can drive their organizations to explore new frontiers in the blockchain space.

The evolving regulatory landscape presents significant challenges for leaders in blockchain. Regulatory frameworks for blockchain and cryptocurrencies are still developing, and organizations must navigate a complex web of compliance requirements. Leaders need to stay informed about regulatory changes and proactively engage with policymakers to shape favorable regulations. Additionally, blockchain raises unique ethical considerations. Issues such as data privacy, security, and the potential for misuse of technology must be addressed thoughtfully. Leaders must establish clear ethical guidelines and ensure that their organizations adhere to best practices in blockchain implementation.

A blockchain leader might need to balance the transparency benefits of blockchain with the need to protect sensitive user information. This requires a nuanced understanding of both the technology and the ethical implications of its use.

Implementing blockchain technology often involves significant changes to existing processes and systems. Leaders must manage these changes effectively to ensure a smooth transition and buy-in from all stakeholders. This involves clear communication about the benefits and challenges of blockchain, as well as a well-thought-out change management strategy.

Building trust is crucial in this process. Leaders must engage with employees, customers, and partners transparently, addressing concerns and demonstrating how blockchain will create value for everyone involved. By involving stakeholders in the implementation process and showing tangible benefits, leaders can build the trust needed for successful adoption.

The rise of blockchain technology necessitates a fundamental shift in traditional leadership models. Leaders must adapt to decentralized decision-making, embrace transparency, adopt adaptive and networked leadership styles, foster a culture of innovation, navigate regulatory and ethical challenges, and build trust while managing change. By evolving their leadership approaches to align with the principles of blockchain, leaders can drive organizational transformation and position their organizations for long-term success in a decentralized future. This understanding of the leadership challenges and opportunities presented by blockchain sets the stage for exploring the broader organizational implications and strategies for successful adoption, which we will discuss in the following sections.

Blockchain technology is driving the emergence of new business models that leverage its unique features, such as decentralization, transparency, and immutability. These new models are disrupting traditional industries and creating opportunities for innovation and growth. One of the most notable new business models enabled by blockchain is the concept of Decentralized Finance, or DeFi. DeFi encompasses a wide range of financial services that operate without traditional intermediaries like banks. Instead, these services are built on blockchain networks using smart contracts, which automate and enforce the terms of financial agreements.

DeFi platforms allow users to lend, borrow, trade, and invest in cryptocurrencies directly with each other. For instance, platforms like Aave and Compound enable users to lend their cryptocurrencies and earn interest or borrow against their holdings. Uniswap and SushiSwap provide decentralized exchanges where users can trade cryptocurrencies without relying on centralized exchanges. These platforms democratize access to financial services, making them available to anyone with an internet connection, and often offer higher returns than traditional financial products.

Another innovative business model is the tokenization of assets. Tokenization involves converting physical or digital assets into digital tokens that can be traded on a blockchain. This process can be applied to a wide range of assets, including real estate, art, commodities, and even intellectual property. Tokenization increases liquidity by allowing fractional ownership and easier transfer of assets. For example, a piece of real estate can be divided into multiple tokens, enabling smaller investors to buy and trade shares of the property. This opens up investment opportunities to a broader audience and can lead to more efficient markets.

Non-fungible tokens (NFTs) represent another groundbreaking business model enabled by blockchain. NFTs are unique digital assets that can represent ownership of digital art, collectibles, music, and other forms of digital media. Unlike cryptocurrencies, which are fungible and can be exchanged on a one-to-one basis, each NFT is unique and cannot be replicated. This uniqueness has created a new market for digital ownership and provenance, allowing artists and creators to monetize their work directly. Platforms like OpenSea and Rarible facilitate the creation, buying, and selling of NFTs, providing new revenue streams for artists and content creators.

Blockchain also supports the development of Decentralized Autonomous Organizations (DAOs), which are organizations governed by smart contracts and operated by a distributed network of participants. DAOs operate on a set of rules encoded on the blockchain, with decisions made through consensus mechanisms. This model eliminates the need for a centralized leadership structure, promoting a more democratic and transparent form of governance. Participants in a DAO typically hold tokens that grant them voting rights, allowing them to influence the organization's direction and decisions. DAOs can be used for a variety of purposes, from managing investment funds to running decentralized projects and initiatives.

The gaming industry is another sector where blockchain is enabling new business models. Blockchain-based games incorporate digital assets that players can own, trade, and monetize. Games like Axie Infinity and Decentraland allow players to earn cryptocurrency by participating in the game, creating a play-to-earn model. These games use blockchain to ensure the scarcity and ownership of in-game assets, giving players real economic value for their time and effort. This model not only enhances player engagement but also creates new revenue streams for game developers.

Supply chain management is also being transformed by blockchain. Traditional supply chains often suffer from inefficiencies and lack of transparency, which can lead to increased costs and risks. Blockchain provides a decentralized ledger that records every transaction and movement of goods, making supply chains more transparent and traceable. For example, companies like IBM and Walmart are using blockchain to track the provenance of food products, ensuring that consumers receive safe and authentic goods. This traceability can be extended to other industries, such as pharmaceuticals and luxury goods, to combat counterfeiting and improve product safety.

Blockchain enables the creation of decentralized marketplaces where buyers and sellers can transact directly without intermediaries. These marketplaces can operate with lower fees and greater transparency compared to traditional platforms. For example, Origin Protocol and OpenBazaar offer decentralized marketplaces for goods and services, allowing users to trade directly with each other using cryptocurrency. This model empowers small businesses and individual sellers by reducing reliance on centralized platforms and intermediaries.

In the energy sector, blockchain is facilitating peer-to-peer energy trading. Traditional energy markets are dominated by large utilities that control the distribution and pricing of energy. Blockchain enables decentralized energy markets where individuals and businesses can trade excess energy directly with each other. Platforms like Power Ledger and Grid+ use blockchain to create transparent and efficient energy markets, promoting renewable energy usage and reducing costs for consumers.

This technology is enabling a wide range of new business models that leverage its decentralized, transparent, and immutable nature. These models are disrupting traditional industries, creating new opportunities for innovation and growth, and empowering individuals and small businesses. By understanding and embracing these new business models, leaders can position their organizations to capitalize on the transformative potential of blockchain, driving innovation and long-term success. This exploration of blockchain-enabled business models sets the stage for examining the organizational implications and strategies for successful adoption, which will be discussed in the following sections.

Embracing decentralized decision-making and distributed authority is crucial for leaders in the blockchain era. Traditional hierarchical structures, where decisions are made by a few individuals at the top, are often inefficient and slow to respond to changes. In contrast, blockchain technology supports a decentralized approach, distributing decision-making authority across a network of participants. This shift can lead to more agile, inclusive, and transparent organizations.

Decentralized decision-making involves distributing authority to a broader group of stakeholders, rather than concentrating power in the hands of a few. In a blockchain-based organization, this means that decisions are often made through consensus mechanisms, where participants vote on proposals and initiatives. This inclusive approach ensures that a diverse range of perspectives is considered, leading to more balanced and well-informed decisions.

For leaders, this transition requires a significant shift in mindset and management style. Instead of acting as top-down decision-makers, leaders must become facilitators who guide and support the decision-making process. This involves fostering an environment where open communication and collaboration are encouraged. Leaders must be adept at managing diverse teams and bringing together different viewpoints to achieve consensus.

One of the key advantages of decentralized decision-making is its ability to increase organizational agility. In traditional hierarchies, decisions can be bogged down by layers of bureaucracy, slowing response times and stifling innovation. Decentralized models, on the other hand, allow organizations to react quickly to changes and opportunities. For example, in a Decentralized Autonomous Organization (DAO), decisions about funding projects or changing protocols can be made swiftly through token-holder votes, enabling the organization to adapt rapidly to market conditions.

Distributed authority also promotes greater accountability and transparency. When decision-making power is shared, it reduces the risk of abuse and corruption that can occur when authority is concentrated. Blockchain's transparent ledger ensures that all decisions and transactions are recorded and visible to all participants, fostering a culture of openness and trust. Leaders must embrace this transparency, making their actions and decisions clear and justifiable to all stakeholders.

To implement decentralized decision-making effectively, leaders need to leverage the right tools and technologies. Blockchain platforms offer various consensus mechanisms, such as Proof of Stake (PoS) and Delegated Proof of Stake (DPoS), which can be used to facilitate fair and efficient decision-making processes. Smart contracts can automate governance rules and ensure that decisions are executed as agreed, reducing the potential for human error and bias.

Training and education are also vital. Leaders must ensure that their teams understand the principles of decentralized decision-making and are comfortable using the technologies that support it. This might involve investing in training programs, workshops, and continuous learning opportunities to build the necessary skills and knowledge.

Leaders must focus on building a strong organizational culture that values collaboration, trust, and shared responsibility. This involves setting clear expectations and creating a supportive environment where team members feel empowered to take initiative and contribute to decision-making processes. Recognizing and rewarding collaborative efforts can further reinforce these values.

In addition to internal organizational changes, leaders must also consider the broader ecosystem. Embracing decentralized decision-making often involves collaborating with external partners, communities, and stakeholders. Building strong networks and alliances is crucial for leveraging the full potential of blockchain technology. Leaders must be skilled in stakeholder management, able to navigate complex relationships and foster cooperation across different groups.

One example of successful decentralized decision-making is the Ethereum blockchain. Ethereum's development is guided by a decentralized community of developers, miners, and users who propose and vote on improvements through the Ethereum Improvement Proposal (EIP) process. This collaborative approach has enabled Ethereum to evolve continuously and maintain its position as a leading blockchain platform.

Another example is the DAO, which operates without a traditional management structure. Decisions within a DAO are made collectively by its members, who hold governance tokens. These tokens grant voting rights, allowing members to influence the organization's direction and decisions. DAOs demonstrate how decentralized decision-making can lead to more democratic and participatory governance models.

Embracing decentralized decision-making and distributed authority is essential for leaders in the blockchain era. This approach promotes agility, inclusivity, transparency, and accountability, positioning organizations to thrive in a rapidly changing environment. Leaders must adapt their management styles, leverage appropriate technologies, invest in education, build a strong organizational culture, and engage with the broader ecosystem. By doing so, they can harness the full potential of blockchain technology and drive their organizations towards innovation and success. This understanding sets the stage for exploring the broader organizational implications and strategies for navigating this transformation, which will be discussed in the following sections.

Increasing transparency in leadership practices is a critical aspect of adapting to the blockchain era. Blockchain technology inherently promotes transparency through its decentralized and immutable ledger, which records all transactions and decisions in a manner that is visible to all participants. This transparency is not only a technical feature but also a catalyst for building enhanced trust within organizations and among stakeholders.

Enhanced trust and transparency through blockchain begin with the technology's core principle: an immutable, decentralized ledger that ensures all transactions are recorded accurately and are accessible to all authorized participants. This means that any action taken within a blockchain-based system can be audited and verified independently, reducing the potential for misinformation or manipulation. For leadership, this translates into a powerful tool for promoting accountability and openness.

In traditional organizations, information is often siloed, and transparency can be limited by hierarchical structures and gatekeeping. Leaders may selectively share information, which can lead to mistrust and speculation among employees and stakeholders. Blockchain disrupts this model by making information consistently available across the network. Every stakeholder, from employees to customers to regulatory bodies, can access the same data, fostering a culture of openness. For example, in financial management, blockchain can be used to create a transparent record of all financial transactions. This ensures that expenditures, investments, and other financial activities are visible and verifiable. Leaders who adopt this level of transparency can demonstrate fiscal responsibility and ethical management, thereby building trust with employees, investors, and other stakeholders. In a practical scenario, a company using blockchain for financial transparency would allow its stakeholders to track how funds are allocated and spent, ensuring that resources are used effectively and ethically.

Blockchain also enhances transparency in supply chain management. Leaders can use blockchain to provide real-time visibility into the sourcing, production, and distribution of goods. This level of transparency is particularly valuable in industries where provenance and authenticity are critical, such as in food safety, pharmaceuticals, and luxury goods. By offering stakeholders clear insights into the entire supply chain, leaders can build trust and ensure that their operations meet ethical and quality standards. For instance, a food company might use blockchain to track every step of its product's journey from farm to table, assuring customers of the product's safety and quality.

Smart contracts further enhance transparency by automating agreements and ensuring they are executed as written. These contracts are self-executing, with the terms directly encoded into the blockchain. This eliminates the need for intermediaries and reduces the risk of human error or intentional manipulation. Leaders can use smart contracts to streamline processes such as procurement, compliance, and performance management. By automating these functions, they provide a clear, tamper-proof record of all actions taken, which can be audited at any time. For example, a company could use a smart contract to automatically manage supplier payments, releasing funds only when goods are delivered and verified, ensuring accountability and trust in the procurement process.

Transparency in decision-making is another area where blockchain can significantly impact leadership practices. In traditional settings, decisions made at the top often lack visibility, leading to questions about fairness and inclusivity. Blockchain can democratize decision-making processes by allowing stakeholders to participate and vote on important issues through decentralized platforms. This not only enhances transparency but also encourages a more inclusive and participatory approach to governance. For instance, a decentralized organization might use a blockchain-based voting system to allow all members to vote on strategic initiatives, ensuring that decisions reflect the collective will of the community.

Blockchain's transparency extends to compliance and regulatory reporting. Organizations can use blockchain to provide regulators with real-time access to transactional data, simplifying compliance and reducing the risk of regulatory breaches. This proactive approach to transparency can enhance an organization's reputation and build trust with regulatory bodies. For example, a financial institution might use blockchain to automatically report transactions to regulatory authorities, ensuring compliance with anti-money laundering (AML) and know-your-customer (KYC) regulations.

In implementing these transparent practices, leaders must also consider the cultural shift required within their organizations. Transparency is not just about making information available; it's about creating an environment where openness is valued and practiced. Leaders should encourage open communication, regularly share insights and updates, and be receptive to feedback. This cultural shift can be supported by blockchain technology but ultimately depends on the commitment and behavior of the leadership team.

Blockchain technology offers a powerful framework for enhancing transparency in leadership practices. By leveraging blockchain's decentralized and immutable ledger, leaders can promote accountability, build trust, and foster a culture of openness within their organizations. Whether it's through financial transparency, supply chain visibility, smart contracts, or inclusive decision-making, blockchain enables leaders to operate more transparently and ethically. Embracing these practices not only strengthens internal trust but also enhances the organization's credibility and reputation with external stakeholders. This sets the stage for the broader organizational transformations necessary for successful blockchain adoption, which will be discussed in the following sections.

The concept of "leadership on a blockchain" represents a transformative shift from traditional hierarchical leadership models to a decentralized, transparent, and collaborative approach. This new leadership paradigm leverages the core principles of blockchain technology—decentralization, transparency, and immutability—to foster a more inclusive, accountable, and adaptive form of governance.

At its core, "leadership on a blockchain" decentralizes decision-making processes. In traditional organizations, decision-making authority is often concentrated at the top, with leaders making choices that are then implemented throughout the organization. This top-down approach can lead to bottlenecks, slow response times, and a lack of diverse perspectives. Blockchain technology, however, enables decision-making to be distributed across a network of participants. This means that important decisions are made collectively, through consensus mechanisms that involve a wider array of stakeholders.

Decentralized Autonomous Organizations (DAOs) embody the principles of "leadership on a blockchain." In a DAO, governance and decision-making are managed through smart contracts on the blockchain. Members of the organization hold tokens that grant them voting rights, allowing them to propose and vote on initiatives, budgets, and policies. This democratic approach ensures that all voices are heard, and decisions reflect the collective will of the community. Leaders in this environment act more as facilitators and coordinators rather than traditional top-down managers.

Transparency is another critical aspect of "leadership on a blockchain." Blockchain's transparent ledger ensures that all actions, decisions, and transactions are recorded and visible to all participants. This level of transparency fosters trust and accountability, as leaders cannot hide or manipulate information. Every decision and its rationale are accessible, which encourages ethical behavior and reduces the risk of corruption.

In practice, this means that leaders must operate with a high degree of openness. They need to communicate clearly and regularly with stakeholders, providing updates and seeking input on key decisions. This transparency extends to financial management, strategic planning, and operational activities, creating an environment where trust is built through openness and honesty.

Immutability, another hallmark of blockchain, ensures that once a decision or transaction is recorded, it cannot be altered or deleted. This permanence adds a layer of security and trust to leadership practices. Leaders cannot retroactively change their decisions or obscure their actions, which enhances accountability. This also means that leaders must be thorough and thoughtful in their decision-making processes, knowing that their actions are permanently recorded and subject to scrutiny.

The collaborative nature of blockchain also shifts leadership dynamics. In traditional settings, leaders often work within siloed structures, with limited cross-functional collaboration. Blockchain, however, thrives on the collective input and cooperation of diverse participants. Leaders must therefore adopt a more networked approach, building strong relationships both within and outside the organization. This involves engaging with a broad range of stakeholders, including employees, customers, partners, and even competitors, to foster innovation and drive shared goals.

For instance, in the blockchain ecosystem, collaboration between different projects and communities is common. Leaders often participate in cross-project initiatives, share knowledge, and co-develop solutions. This collaborative spirit is essential for driving the rapid innovation and adaptability that blockchain technology demands.

"Leadership on a blockchain" also requires a focus on continuous learning and adaptation. The blockchain space is rapidly evolving, with new technologies, regulations, and market dynamics emerging constantly. Leaders must stay informed about these changes and be willing to adapt their strategies accordingly. This involves not only keeping up with technical advancements but also understanding broader trends and shifts in the industry.

To thrive in this environment, leaders should encourage a culture of learning within their organizations. This means providing opportunities for team members to upskill, experiment with new technologies, and stay engaged with industry developments. By fostering a learning-oriented culture, leaders can ensure that their organizations remain agile and resilient in the face of change. Moreover, ethical considerations are paramount in "leadership on a blockchain." The transparent and immutable nature of blockchain amplifies the importance of ethical leadership. Leaders must navigate complex issues related to privacy, security, and the potential misuse of technology. Establishing and adhering to clear ethical guidelines is crucial. Leaders must set the tone for ethical behavior, ensuring that their organizations prioritize responsible and fair use of blockchain technology.

The concept of "leadership on a blockchain" represents a fundamental shift towards a more decentralized, transparent, and collaborative approach to leadership. By embracing these principles, leaders can foster greater trust, accountability, and innovation within their organizations. This new leadership paradigm challenges traditional models, requiring leaders to adapt their practices and mindsets to leverage the full potential of blockchain technology. As organizations navigate this transformation, the role of leaders will be crucial in guiding their teams through the complexities and opportunities of the blockchain era. This exploration of leadership on a blockchain sets the stage for discussing the broader organizational transformations necessary for successful blockchain adoption, which we will explore in the following sections.

Promoting networked, collaborative, and adaptive leadership styles is essential for successfully navigating the decentralized and dynamic environment created by blockchain technology. These leadership styles align closely with the core principles of blockchain and are crucial for fostering innovation, agility, and resilience within organizations.

Networked leadership emphasizes the importance of building and maintaining strong relationships across different groups and stakeholders. In the context of blockchain, where ecosystems are often decentralized and interdependent, leaders must be adept at creating and sustaining networks both within and outside their organizations. This involves engaging with a diverse array of participants, including employees, customers, partners, regulatory bodies, and other industry players.

A networked leader in a blockchain organization might actively participate in industry forums, collaborate on open-source projects, and form alliances with other blockchain initiatives. By leveraging these networks, leaders can gain access to a wealth of knowledge, resources, and opportunities that can drive their organization's growth and innovation. This interconnected approach ensures that leaders are not working in isolation but are instead part of a broader ecosystem that supports and enhances their efforts.

Collaborative leadership, meanwhile, focuses on fostering a culture of teamwork and collective problem-solving. Blockchain's decentralized nature inherently encourages collaboration, as it requires consensus and collective input to function effectively. Leaders must therefore create environments where collaboration is valued and facilitated.

This can be achieved by implementing structures and practices that promote open communication, knowledge sharing, and joint decision-making. For instance, leaders can establish cross-functional teams that bring together individuals with diverse skills and perspectives to work on blockchain projects. By encouraging employees to collaborate and contribute their unique insights, leaders can drive more innovative and effective solutions.

Collaborative leadership also involves empowering team members to take ownership of their work and make decisions. In a blockchain context, this might mean giving developers and engineers more autonomy to experiment with new ideas and technologies. By decentralizing authority and encouraging a sense of ownership, leaders can foster a more engaged and motivated workforce.

Adaptive leadership is crucial in the rapidly evolving blockchain landscape. The pace of technological change, coupled with the emergence of new market dynamics and regulatory frameworks, requires leaders to be flexible and responsive. Adaptive leaders are those who can pivot quickly in response to new information and changing circumstances, ensuring their organizations remain competitive and resilient.

To promote adaptive leadership, leaders should cultivate a mindset of continuous learning and experimentation within their organizations. This involves staying informed about the latest developments in blockchain technology and being willing to explore new approaches and strategies. Leaders should also encourage their teams to experiment and take calculated risks, learning from both successes and failures. For instance, an adaptive leader in a blockchain company might pilot new technologies or business models in a controlled environment before scaling them across the organization. By continuously testing and refining their approaches, adaptive leaders can identify the most effective strategies and quickly respond to emerging trends and opportunities.

Another key aspect of adaptive leadership is resilience. Blockchain projects can be complex and often face unexpected challenges, such as regulatory changes or technical setbacks. Adaptive leaders must be able to navigate these challenges with resilience, maintaining focus on long-term goals while being flexible enough to adjust tactics as needed. This involves fostering a culture where challenges are viewed as opportunities for learning and growth, rather than as insurmountable obstacles.

Building an organization that embraces networked, collaborative, and adaptive leadership styles requires deliberate effort and strategic planning. Leaders should invest in the tools and technologies that facilitate these leadership styles, such as collaboration platforms, communication tools, and data analytics systems. These tools can enhance connectivity, streamline collaboration, and provide the insights needed to make informed, adaptive decisions.

Training and development programs are also essential. Leaders should provide opportunities for employees to develop the skills needed for effective collaboration and adaptation, such as communication, problem-solving, and critical thinking. This might involve workshops, mentoring programs, and continuous learning initiatives that keep employees engaged and up-to-date with the latest industry trends.

Cultural transformation is another critical component. Leaders must model the behaviors they wish to see in their teams, demonstrating openness, flexibility, and a commitment to collaboration. By consistently reinforcing these values and recognizing collaborative and adaptive efforts, leaders can embed these principles into the organizational culture.

Promoting networked, collaborative, and adaptive leadership styles is vital for leveraging the full potential of blockchain technology. Networked leadership builds strong relationships across the ecosystem, collaborative leadership fosters teamwork and collective problem-solving, and adaptive leadership ensures flexibility and resilience in a rapidly changing environment. By embracing these leadership styles, leaders can drive innovation, enhance organizational agility, and position their organizations for long-term success in the blockchain era. This comprehensive approach to leadership transformation sets the stage for the broader organizational changes necessary for successful blockchain adoption, which will be discussed in the following sections.

# Chapter 4: Organizational Transformation

Adopting blockchain technology brings profound organizational implications, requiring significant shifts in structure, processes, culture, and governance. To leverage the full potential of blockchain, organizations must undergo a transformation that aligns their operations with the principles of decentralization, transparency, and efficiency inherent in blockchain systems.

One of the most immediate implications is the need for structural change. Traditional hierarchical structures, where decision-making authority is centralized, are often at odds with the decentralized nature of blockchain. Organizations must consider flattening their hierarchies to foster more distributed decision-making processes. This shift can involve creating decentralized units or teams that operate autonomously while staying aligned with the organization's overall goals. For example, a company might establish cross-functional teams empowered to make decisions on blockchain projects independently, thereby increasing agility and responsiveness.

Process reengineering is another critical area affected by blockchain adoption. Traditional business processes often involve multiple intermediaries and complex workflows that can be streamlined through blockchain technology. Processes such as supply chain management, financial transactions, and contract execution can be automated and made more efficient using smart contracts. This automation not only reduces operational costs but also minimizes the risk of errors and fraud. For instance, a supply chain company might implement a blockchain solution to track the movement of goods from production to delivery, ensuring real-time visibility and accountability at each stage.

The adoption of blockchain technology also necessitates a cultural shift within organizations. The transparency and immutability of blockchain require a culture that values openness, ethical behavior, and accountability. Employees and leaders alike must be comfortable with increased visibility into their actions and decisions. Cultivating a culture of transparency involves encouraging open communication, promoting ethical conduct, and establishing clear guidelines for behavior. Leaders must lead by example, demonstrating a commitment to these values and fostering an environment where employees feel empowered to act with integrity.

Governance models must also evolve to accommodate blockchain's decentralized nature. Traditional governance often relies on centralized oversight and control, which can be inefficient and prone to bottlenecks. Blockchain enables new governance frameworks, such as Decentralized Autonomous Organizations (DAOs), where decision-making is distributed among stakeholders through token-based voting mechanisms. These models promote inclusivity and democratize organizational control, ensuring that all voices are heard and valued. Implementing such governance structures requires careful planning and the establishment of clear rules and protocols to guide decision-making processes.

Talent and skill development are crucial for successful blockchain adoption. Blockchain technology is complex and rapidly evolving, necessitating a workforce that is knowledgeable and adaptable. Organizations must invest in training and development programs to equip their employees with the necessary skills. This includes not only technical skills related to blockchain development and implementation but also soft skills such as critical thinking, problem-solving, and collaboration. By fostering a culture of continuous learning, organizations can ensure that their teams remain competitive and capable of driving innovation.

Security and privacy are paramount considerations when adopting blockchain. While blockchain technology offers enhanced security features through cryptographic methods and decentralized storage, it also introduces new challenges. Organizations must develop robust security strategies to protect their blockchain networks from threats such as hacking and fraud. This involves implementing advanced cybersecurity measures, conducting regular audits, and educating employees about best practices for data protection. Additionally, privacy concerns must be addressed, particularly in industries handling sensitive information such as healthcare and finance. Organizations need to balance the transparency benefits of blockchain with the need to protect personal and proprietary data.

Regulatory compliance is another critical area impacted by blockchain adoption. The regulatory landscape for blockchain and cryptocurrencies is still evolving, and organizations must navigate complex and often uncertain regulatory environments. Compliance with laws and regulations, such as anti-money laundering (AML) and know-your-customer (KYC) requirements, is essential to avoid legal pitfalls and maintain operational integrity. Organizations must stay informed about regulatory developments and engage with policymakers to help shape favorable regulatory frameworks. Establishing a compliance team or working with legal experts who specialize in blockchain can help organizations manage regulatory risks effectively.

Integration with existing systems is a practical challenge that organizations face when adopting blockchain. Many organizations have legacy systems that may not be directly compatible with blockchain technology. Integrating blockchain with these existing systems requires careful planning and execution to ensure seamless interoperability. This might involve developing custom APIs, using middleware solutions, or gradually transitioning processes to blockchain platforms. Effective integration ensures that organizations can leverage blockchain's benefits without disrupting their ongoing operations.

Change management is essential to guide organizations through the transition to blockchain technology. Implementing blockchain can be disruptive, and resistance to change is common. Leaders must develop a comprehensive change management strategy that includes clear communication, stakeholder engagement, and ongoing support. This involves explaining the benefits of blockchain, addressing concerns, and providing resources to help employees adapt to new workflows and technologies. Successful change management fosters a positive attitude towards blockchain adoption and ensures a smoother transition.

Several organizations have successfully navigated the organizational transformation required for blockchain adoption. For instance, IBM has integrated blockchain into its supply chain management to enhance transparency and efficiency. By creating a blockchain-based network, IBM has improved traceability, reduced fraud, and streamlined processes, demonstrating the practical benefits of blockchain technology in a large enterprise setting.

Another example is the De Beers Group, which uses blockchain to track the provenance of diamonds. Their blockchain platform, Tracr, records each step of a diamond's journey from mine to retail. This transparency ensures the authenticity and ethical sourcing of diamonds, addressing consumer concerns and regulatory requirements. De Beers' implementation of blockchain showcases how the technology can transform traditional industries by providing greater visibility and trust.

In the public sector, the government of Dubai has launched the Dubai Blockchain Strategy, aiming to become the first blockchain-powered city by 2020. This initiative involves implementing blockchain across various government services, including health records, property transactions, and business registrations. Dubai's strategy highlights the potential for blockchain to enhance public administration by improving efficiency, reducing costs, and increasing transparency.

Adopting blockchain technology has profound organizational implications that require significant changes in structure, processes, culture, and governance. By embracing these changes and fostering a culture of transparency, accountability, and continuous learning, organizations can successfully navigate the transition to blockchain and leverage its transformative potential. The following sections will delve deeper into the strategies for managing this transformation, including fostering a blockchain-friendly organizational culture and integrating blockchain into existing systems and processes. Adopting blockchain technology necessitates profound cultural shifts and the development of new governance models. These changes are essential to fully leverage the potential of blockchain and align organizational practices with its core principles of decentralization, transparency, and collaboration.

Implementing blockchain technology requires a significant transformation in organizational culture. Traditional corporate cultures often emphasize hierarchy, control, and siloed information. Blockchain, however, thrives on principles of decentralization, openness, and collective responsibility. For blockchain adoption to be successful, organizations must foster a culture that embraces these principles.

A key aspect of this cultural shift is the move towards greater transparency. In a blockchain-enabled environment, transparency is not just a technical feature but a cultural imperative. Organizations must cultivate an environment where open communication is encouraged, and information is freely shared across all levels. Leaders should model transparency by sharing their decisions, rationales, and results openly, setting the tone for the rest of the organization.

Trust and Accountability are also crucial cultural elements. Blockchain's immutable ledger holds all actions and transactions to public scrutiny, making accountability a foundational aspect. Organizations must nurture a culture where trust is built through consistent and ethical behavior. Employees should feel empowered to take responsibility for their actions, knowing that their contributions are visible and valued. This involves creating clear ethical guidelines and ensuring that everyone in the organization understands and adheres to them.

Collaboration is another critical cultural shift. Blockchain projects often require input from a wide range of stakeholders, including developers, business leaders, regulators, and customers. This necessitates a culture that values teamwork and collective problem-solving. Leaders should encourage cross-functional collaboration and create opportunities for employees to work together on blockchain initiatives. This can be facilitated through regular team meetings, collaborative tools, and a physical or virtual environment that supports teamwork.

Innovation and Continuous Learning must be ingrained in the organizational culture to keep pace with the rapidly evolving blockchain landscape. This involves fostering a mindset that embraces change and views challenges as opportunities for growth. Organizations should invest in training and development programs that keep employees up-to-date with the latest blockchain advancements and industry trends. Encouraging experimentation and allowing room for failure can also drive innovation, as employees feel safe to explore new ideas and approaches.

The decentralized nature of blockchain necessitates the development of new governance models that move away from traditional centralized control. These models are designed to be more inclusive, democratic, and efficient, aligning with the principles of blockchain technology.

One such model is the Decentralized Autonomous Organization (DAO). In a DAO, decision-making power is distributed among the members, typically through a system of token-based voting. Each token holder has a say in the governance of the organization, and decisions are made based on majority consensus. This model ensures that all members have a voice in the organization's direction and operations, promoting inclusivity and collective responsibility. For instance, decisions about project funding, protocol changes, or strategic initiatives in a DAO are proposed and voted on by the community, ensuring that the collective will drives the organization.

Smart Contracts play a crucial role in new governance models. These self-executing contracts have the terms of the agreement directly written into code, which automatically executes when predetermined conditions are met. Smart contracts can be used to enforce governance rules, automate decision-making processes, and ensure compliance with organizational policies. For example, a smart contract could be used to automate the release of funds for a project once specific milestones are achieved, ensuring transparency and accountability in financial management.

The concept of Holacracy is another governance model that aligns well with blockchain principles. Holacracy replaces traditional management hierarchies with a system of self-organizing teams or circles. Each circle operates autonomously and is responsible for specific functions within the organization. Decisions are made through a structured process that involves all members of the circle, promoting decentralized control and collaboration. This model can enhance agility and innovation by empowering teams to make decisions quickly and respond to changes in the environment.

Implementing these new governance models requires careful planning and a willingness to experiment. Organizations must establish clear protocols and guidelines to ensure that decentralized decision-making processes are effective and efficient. This might involve creating detailed governance frameworks that outline the roles, responsibilities, and decision-making processes within the organization. Regular audits and reviews can help ensure that these processes are working as intended and identify areas for improvement.

Several organizations have successfully implemented new governance models to support their blockchain initiatives. For example, Aragon, a platform for building and managing DAOs, provides tools for organizations to create decentralized governance structures. Aragon itself operates as a DAO, with community members voting on key decisions and initiatives. This model has enabled Aragon to remain agile and responsive to the needs of its community while ensuring that governance is transparent and democratic.

Another example is MakerDAO, a decentralized finance platform that operates using a DAO governance model. MakerDAO token holders participate in governance by voting on changes to the protocol, such as adjustments to the stability fee or the addition of new collateral types. This decentralized governance structure has allowed MakerDAO to adapt quickly to market conditions and maintain the stability of its DAI stablecoin.

In the public sector, the city of Zug in Switzerland, also known as "Crypto Valley," has adopted blockchain-based governance models to enhance public services. Zug uses a blockchain-based voting system for local elections and referendums, ensuring transparency and security in the voting process. This initiative demonstrates how new governance models can be applied to public administration to improve efficiency and trust.

Adopting blockchain technology requires significant cultural shifts and the development of new governance models. Organizations must foster a culture of transparency, trust, collaboration, and innovation to fully leverage the potential of blockchain. New governance models, such as DAOs, smart contracts, and holacracy, align with the decentralized nature of blockchain and promote inclusive, democratic, and efficient decision-making. By embracing these cultural and governance changes, organizations can successfully navigate the transition to blockchain and drive long-term success in a decentralized future. This comprehensive understanding sets the stage for exploring strategies for integrating blockchain into existing systems and processes, which will be discussed in the following sections.

Espousing this technology can significantly streamline processes and deliver substantial efficiency gains across various organizational functions. By automating transactions, reducing the need for intermediaries, and enhancing data integrity, blockchain can transform how businesses operate, leading to cost savings, faster execution times, and improved overall performance.

One of the primary ways blockchain enhances efficiency is through the use of smart contracts. Smart contracts are self-executing contracts with the terms of the agreement directly written into code. These contracts automatically execute and enforce themselves when predefined conditions are met, eliminating the need for manual intervention and reducing the risk of errors.

In supply chain management, smart contracts can automate the entire procurement process. When goods are delivered and verified, the smart contract can automatically trigger payment to the supplier. This automation reduces delays and ensures timely payments, improving cash flow management for both parties. Similarly, in insurance, smart contracts can automate claims processing, automatically disbursing funds when specific criteria are met, thereby reducing processing times and administrative costs.

Blockchain's decentralized nature allows for direct peer-to-peer transactions, reducing or even eliminating the need for intermediaries. Traditional business processes often involve multiple intermediaries, each adding time, cost, and complexity to transactions. By removing these intermediaries, blockchain can streamline processes and enhance efficiency.

In financial services, for instance, blockchain can facilitate direct cross-border payments without the need for correspondent banks. Traditional international payments can take several days and incur high fees due to the involvement of multiple banks. Blockchain-based payment systems, like Ripple, enable instant and low-cost transactions by directly connecting the parties involved. This not only speeds up the process but also significantly reduces transaction costs.

Blockchain's immutable ledger ensures that all data recorded on the blockchain is accurate, transparent, and tamper-proof. This high level of data integrity enhances trust and reduces the need for redundant verification processes.

In industries such as healthcare, blockchain can improve data management by providing a single, secure source of truth for patient records. Healthcare providers often struggle with fragmented and inconsistent data across different systems. Blockchain can consolidate patient records into a unified, immutable ledger accessible to authorized healthcare providers. This streamlines patient care by ensuring that all providers have access to the same accurate and up-to-date information, reducing the need for repeated tests and improving the overall efficiency of the healthcare system.

Blockchain enables real-time tracking and monitoring of assets and transactions, providing organizations with greater visibility and control over their operations. In supply chains, blockchain can track the movement of goods from production to delivery in real time. This transparency allows organizations to quickly identify and address any issues, such as delays or quality problems, minimizing disruptions and enhancing efficiency. For example, Walmart uses blockchain to track the provenance of food products. By recording each step of the food supply chain on the blockchain, Walmart can quickly trace the source of any contamination, reducing the time and cost associated with food recalls. This real-time tracking capability enhances food safety and operational efficiency.

Compliance and auditing processes can be time-consuming and costly, often involving extensive documentation and verification. Blockchain's transparent and immutable ledger simplifies these processes by providing a clear and verifiable record of all transactions.

In the financial industry, for example, regulatory compliance requires detailed record-keeping and regular audits. Blockchain can automate compliance reporting by recording all transactions on a transparent ledger that regulators can access in real time. This reduces the administrative burden on financial institutions and enhances the accuracy and reliability of compliance reports.

Similarly, in manufacturing, blockchain can streamline compliance with quality and safety standards. By recording every step of the production process on the blockchain, manufacturers can provide verifiable proof of compliance with regulatory requirements. This simplifies the auditing process and reduces the risk of non-compliance penalties.

Blockchain technology can optimize resource management by improving the accuracy and efficiency of inventory tracking and asset management. In sectors such as retail and manufacturing, maintaining optimal inventory levels is crucial for reducing costs and meeting customer demand. This technology can provide real-time visibility into inventory levels across multiple locations, enabling organizations to manage their stock more effectively. For instance, a retailer using blockchain can track the movement of goods from warehouses to stores, ensuring that inventory levels are balanced and reducing the risk of overstocking or stockouts. This enhanced inventory management capability leads to more efficient use of resources and better customer service.

Blockchain can also streamline processes in the energy sector by facilitating decentralized energy markets. Traditional energy markets are often centralized, with a few large utilities controlling the production and distribution of energy. Blockchain enables peer-to-peer energy trading, where individuals and businesses can buy and sell excess energy directly with each other.

Platforms like Power Ledger use blockchain to create transparent and efficient energy markets. Participants can trade energy in real time, optimizing the use of renewable energy sources and reducing reliance on centralized utilities. This decentralized approach to energy management enhances efficiency, reduces costs, and promotes sustainable energy practices.

Several organizations have successfully implemented blockchain to streamline processes and achieve efficiency gains. For example, the global shipping giant Maersk partnered with IBM to create TradeLens, a blockchain-based platform for supply chain management. TradeLens digitizes and automates the entire shipping process, from documentation to tracking, resulting in faster and more efficient logistics operations. By providing real-time visibility into shipments, TradeLens reduces delays, lowers costs, and improves the overall efficiency of global trade.

Another example is HSBC, which used blockchain to streamline its trade finance operations. Traditional trade finance processes are paper-intensive and time-consuming, involving multiple parties and intermediaries. By using blockchain, HSBC was able to digitize trade documents and automate transactions, reducing processing times from days to hours and significantly cutting operational costs.

In the diamond industry, De Beers implemented a blockchain platform called Tracr to track the provenance of diamonds. By recording each step of a diamond's journey on the blockchain, De Beers ensures the authenticity and ethical sourcing of its products. This transparency not only enhances consumer trust but also streamlines the certification process, reducing administrative overhead.

Blockchain technology offers significant potential for streamlining processes and achieving efficiency gains across various organizational functions. By automating transactions with smart contracts, reducing the need for intermediaries, enhancing data integrity, enabling real-time tracking, and simplifying compliance and resource management, blockchain can transform how businesses operate. Organizations that embrace these capabilities can realize substantial cost savings, faster execution times, and improved overall performance, positioning themselves for success in an increasingly competitive landscape. This understanding of streamlined processes and efficiency gains sets the stage for exploring strategies for integrating blockchain into existing systems and processes, which will be discussed in the following sections.

Integrating blockchain into existing systems and processes requires careful planning, strategic execution, and a willingness to adapt to new ways of working. Organizations must assess their current infrastructure and identify areas where blockchain can add value, such as enhancing security, improving transparency, or streamlining operations. This assessment involves evaluating the compatibility of legacy systems with blockchain technology and determining the most effective integration approach.

A phased approach can be beneficial, starting with pilot projects that test blockchain applications in specific areas before scaling up. This allows organizations to identify potential challenges and refine their strategies. For instance, a company might begin by using blockchain to track a single product line in its supply chain, gradually expanding to other lines as the system proves its effectiveness.

Interoperability is a key consideration in blockchain integration. Organizations need to ensure that their blockchain solution can seamlessly interact with existing systems and databases. This might involve developing custom APIs or using middleware to facilitate communication between blockchain networks and traditional IT infrastructure. Ensuring interoperability helps avoid disruptions and enables a smooth transition.

Data migration is another critical aspect. Organizations must determine how to transfer data from legacy systems to the blockchain securely and efficiently. This process should maintain data integrity and minimize downtime. Establishing clear protocols for data migration, including validation and backup procedures, ensures a reliable transfer of information.

Employee training and engagement are essential for successful blockchain integration. Employees need to understand how blockchain works and how it will impact their roles and responsibilities. Providing comprehensive training programs helps build the necessary skills and knowledge. Involving employees in the integration process fosters a sense of ownership and eases the transition.

Security measures must be enhanced to protect blockchain networks from potential threats. While blockchain offers inherent security advantages, such as cryptographic protection and decentralization, organizations still need to implement robust cybersecurity practices. This includes regular security audits, encryption of sensitive data, and multi-factor authentication to prevent unauthorized access.

Compliance with regulatory requirements is another critical consideration. The regulatory landscape for blockchain is continually evolving, and organizations must stay informed about relevant laws and regulations. This involves working closely with legal experts to ensure that the blockchain implementation meets all compliance standards and does not expose the organization to legal risks.

Scalability is a significant factor in blockchain integration. Organizations must choose a blockchain platform that can handle their current and future transaction volumes. This might involve selecting a blockchain with high throughput capabilities or exploring layer-2 scaling solutions to enhance performance. Ensuring scalability prevents bottlenecks and supports the organization's growth.

Performance monitoring and continuous improvement are vital post-integration. Organizations should establish metrics to evaluate the performance of their blockchain solution, such as transaction speed, cost savings, and user satisfaction. Regularly reviewing these metrics helps identify areas for improvement and ensures that the blockchain implementation continues to deliver value.

Stakeholder communication is crucial throughout the integration process. Keeping stakeholders informed about the progress, benefits, and challenges of blockchain integration fosters transparency and builds trust. This includes regular updates to employees, customers, suppliers, and investors, highlighting how blockchain enhances the organization's capabilities.

Change management strategies should be implemented to address resistance and ensure a smooth transition. This involves clear communication about the reasons for adopting blockchain, the benefits it brings, and how it aligns with the organization's goals. Providing support and resources to help employees adapt to new processes and systems is essential for successful change management.

Collaboration with technology partners can enhance the integration process. Working with experienced blockchain developers and consultants provides valuable insights and technical expertise. These partners can assist with system design, implementation, and troubleshooting, ensuring a robust and effective integration. Case studies from organizations that have successfully integrated blockchain can provide valuable lessons and best practices. For example, IBM's integration of blockchain into its supply chain management demonstrates how a phased approach and strong stakeholder communication can lead to successful implementation. Learning from such examples helps organizations anticipate challenges and develop effective strategies.

Integrating blockchain into existing systems and processes requires a comprehensive and strategic approach. By assessing current infrastructure, ensuring interoperability, managing data migration, enhancing security, complying with regulations, and fostering employee engagement, organizations can achieve a smooth and successful transition. Continuous performance monitoring, effective change management, and collaboration with technology partners further support the integration process, positioning organizations to fully leverage the transformative potential of blockchain technology.

Successfully managing change and fostering a blockchain-friendly organizational culture involves strategic planning, clear communication, and active engagement. The first step is developing a comprehensive change management strategy that outlines the goals, benefits, and implementation plan for blockchain adoption. This strategy should be communicated effectively to all employees, emphasizing how blockchain aligns with the organization's vision and objectives.

Leaders play a crucial role in this transition by modeling openness and transparency. They should share regular updates on the progress of blockchain initiatives, highlighting successes and addressing challenges. Involving employees early in the process helps build a sense of ownership and reduces resistance. This can be achieved through workshops, town hall meetings, and feedback sessions where employees can voice their concerns and contribute ideas.

Training and education are essential to equip employees with the necessary skills and knowledge. Offering comprehensive training programs that cover the basics of blockchain technology, its applications, and its impact on specific roles within the organization ensures that everyone is prepared for the changes ahead. Continuous learning opportunities, such as online courses and certification programs, help employees stay updated on the latest developments in blockchain technology.

Creating a supportive environment where experimentation and innovation are encouraged is vital. This involves providing resources and tools that allow employees to explore blockchain applications relevant to their work. Leaders should recognize and reward innovative efforts, fostering a culture where taking calculated risks is seen as a path to growth and improvement.

Collaboration and teamwork are also critical. Establishing cross-functional teams that bring together diverse skill sets and perspectives can drive successful blockchain projects. These teams should be empowered to make decisions and take ownership of their initiatives, promoting a sense of responsibility and accountability.

Engaging with external partners and the broader blockchain community can provide valuable insights and support. Collaborating with blockchain experts, consultants, and technology providers can enhance the organization's capabilities and accelerate the adoption process. Participation in industry forums, conferences, and networking events helps build connections and stay informed about emerging trends and best practices.

Maintaining a focus on the ethical implications of blockchain technology is important for building trust and ensuring responsible use. Leaders should establish clear guidelines on ethical behavior and data privacy, ensuring that all blockchain applications comply with relevant regulations and standards. This commitment to ethical practices enhances the organization's reputation and fosters stakeholder trust.

Monitoring and evaluating the impact of blockchain initiatives is crucial for continuous improvement. Establishing metrics to assess the effectiveness of blockchain implementations, such as efficiency gains, cost savings, and employee satisfaction, provides valuable feedback. Regularly reviewing these metrics helps identify areas for refinement and ensures that the organization continues to benefit from its blockchain investments.

Effective change management also involves addressing resistance and fostering a positive attitude towards the transition. Clear and consistent communication about the benefits of blockchain, along with addressing any misconceptions or fears, helps mitigate resistance. Providing support resources, such as help desks or peer support groups, can assist employees in adapting to new processes and systems.

Building a culture that values transparency, collaboration, and continuous learning is key to fostering a blockchain-friendly organization. Leaders should encourage open dialogue, celebrate successes, and learn from failures. By creating an inclusive environment where everyone feels valued and empowered, organizations can harness the full potential of blockchain technology and drive sustained innovation and growth.

Several organizations have successfully undergone blockchain-driven transformation, showcasing the diverse applications and benefits of the technology across different industries. These case studies highlight how blockchain can streamline processes, enhance transparency, and drive innovation.

One notable example is IBM's integration of blockchain into its supply chain management. IBM developed the IBM Food Trust, a blockchain-based platform that enhances food traceability and safety. By recording every step of the food supply chain on a transparent and immutable ledger, IBM Food Trust allows participants to track the origin and journey of food products in real time. This not only improves food safety by enabling rapid identification of contamination sources but also increases efficiency by reducing the time and cost associated with traditional record-keeping methods. The platform's success has attracted numerous industry partners, including Walmart and Nestlé, who use it to ensure the authenticity and quality of their products.

In the diamond industry, De Beers has implemented a blockchain platform called Tracr to enhance the traceability and authenticity of diamonds. Tracr records the journey of each diamond from the mine to the retail market, ensuring that consumers can verify the origin and ethical sourcing of their purchases. This blockchain solution addresses issues of fraud and conflict diamonds by providing a transparent and tamper-proof record of a diamond's provenance. By leveraging blockchain technology, De Beers has strengthened consumer trust and streamlined the certification process, reducing administrative overhead and enhancing operational efficiency.

The financial services sector has also seen significant blockchain adoption. HSBC, a global banking giant, utilized blockchain to streamline its trade finance operations. Traditionally, trade finance processes are paper-intensive and time-consuming, involving multiple parties and intermediaries. HSBC implemented a blockchain-based solution that digitizes trade documents and automates transactions. This integration has reduced processing times from days to hours and significantly lowered operational costs. By enhancing transparency and efficiency, HSBC's blockchain initiative has improved the overall trade finance experience for its clients.

In the public sector, the government of Dubai launched the Dubai Blockchain Strategy with the aim of becoming the first blockchain-powered city. This initiative involves implementing blockchain technology across various government services, including health records, property transactions, and business registrations. For instance, the Dubai Land Department uses blockchain to record real estate transactions, making the process more transparent, secure, and efficient. The strategy also includes a blockchain-based digital identity system, which streamlines access to government services for residents. By leveraging blockchain, Dubai has improved the efficiency and transparency of its public administration, setting a precedent for other cities and governments to follow.

The automotive industry has also embraced blockchain for enhancing supply chain transparency and efficiency. Volvo, for example, uses blockchain to trace the supply chain of cobalt used in its electric vehicle batteries. By recording each step of the cobalt supply chain on a blockchain, Volvo ensures that the materials are sourced responsibly and ethically. This transparency not only enhances consumer trust but also helps Volvo comply with regulatory requirements related to ethical sourcing and environmental sustainability.

In healthcare, MedRec, developed by MIT, uses blockchain technology to create a decentralized record-keeping system for patient data. MedRec allows patients to manage access to their medical records, ensuring that healthcare providers have accurate and up-to-date information. This blockchain solution addresses the issue of fragmented patient data and enhances data security and interoperability. By providing a single, tamper-proof source of truth for patient records, MedRec improves the quality of care and reduces administrative burdens on healthcare providers.

The energy sector has seen innovative applications of blockchain as well. Power Ledger, an Australian company, developed a blockchain platform that enables peer-to-peer energy trading. This platform allows individuals and businesses to buy and sell excess renewable energy directly with each other, bypassing traditional energy utilities. By facilitating transparent and efficient energy transactions, Power Ledger promotes the use of renewable energy sources and reduces energy costs for consumers. The platform's success has led to pilot projects in various countries, showcasing the potential of blockchain to transform the energy market.

These case studies illustrate the transformative potential of blockchain technology across different industries. Organizations that have successfully implemented blockchain solutions have achieved significant benefits, including enhanced transparency, improved efficiency, and increased trust among stakeholders. By leveraging blockchain's unique capabilities, these organizations have not only addressed specific industry challenges but also set new standards for innovation and operational excellence. These examples provide valuable insights and lessons for other organizations seeking to undergo blockchain-driven transformation, demonstrating the wide-ranging applications and benefits of this revolutionary technology.

# Chapter 5: Regulatory and Legal Considerations

Blockchain technology, while revolutionary, presents significant regulatory and legal challenges that organizations must navigate to ensure compliant and secure implementation. These challenges stem from the decentralized, immutable, and often pseudonymous nature of blockchain, which can complicate traditional regulatory frameworks designed for centralized systems.

One of the primary regulatory challenges is compliance with existing laws and regulations. Blockchain technology often intersects with various legal domains, including finance, data protection, and contract law. For example, financial institutions using blockchain must adhere to anti-money laundering (AML) and know-your-customer (KYC) regulations, which require detailed verification of participants in financial transactions. The pseudonymous nature of many blockchain platforms can make it difficult to identify and verify users, complicating compliance with these regulations.

Data privacy is another critical challenge. Regulations like the General Data Protection Regulation (GDPR) in Europe impose strict requirements on the collection, storage, and processing of personal data. Blockchain's immutable ledger, where data cannot be easily altered or deleted, can conflict with GDPR provisions such as the right to be forgotten. Organizations must find ways to comply with data privacy laws while leveraging blockchain's benefits, which might involve using encryption techniques or off-chain storage solutions to protect personal information.

Securities regulation is particularly relevant for blockchain projects that involve the issuance of tokens. Regulatory bodies, such as the U.S. Securities and Exchange Commission (SEC), have classified certain tokens as securities, subjecting them to stringent regulatory requirements. Initial Coin Offerings (ICOs) and Security Token Offerings (STOs) must comply with securities laws, including registration and disclosure requirements. Navigating these regulations requires a clear understanding of the legal status of tokens and careful structuring of token offerings to avoid regulatory pitfalls.

Jurisdictional challenges arise because blockchain operates on a global scale, transcending national boundaries. Different countries have varying regulatory approaches to blockchain and cryptocurrencies, leading to a fragmented legal landscape. Organizations must ensure compliance with the regulations of all jurisdictions in which they operate, which can be complex and resource-intensive. This challenge is compounded by the fact that regulatory frameworks are continually evolving, requiring organizations to stay informed about changes and adapt their strategies accordingly.

Intellectual property rights are also impacted by blockchain technology. The decentralized and open-source nature of many blockchain platforms can complicate the protection and enforcement of intellectual property. Organizations must navigate issues related to the ownership of blockchain code, patents for blockchain innovations, and the licensing of blockchain-based software. Establishing clear intellectual property policies and engaging with legal experts in blockchain IP can help mitigate these risks.

Smart contracts, which are self-executing contracts with the terms directly written into code, present unique legal challenges. While smart contracts can automate and enforce agreements, they also raise questions about enforceability, legal recognition, and liability. For example, determining which jurisdiction's laws apply to a smart contract executed across multiple countries can be complicated. Additionally, issues can arise if the smart contract code contains errors or if unforeseen circumstances impact the contract's execution. Organizations must work with legal professionals to draft smart contracts that are legally sound and include provisions for dispute resolution.

Taxation is another critical area of concern. The taxation of blockchain transactions, including cryptocurrency trading, mining rewards, and token offerings, varies significantly across jurisdictions. Organizations must understand the tax implications of their blockchain activities and ensure accurate reporting and compliance. This may involve working with tax advisors who specialize in cryptocurrency and blockchain taxation.

To address these regulatory and legal challenges, organizations should develop comprehensive compliance strategies. This involves staying informed about relevant regulations, engaging with regulatory bodies, and participating in industry groups that advocate for favorable regulatory frameworks. Establishing a dedicated compliance team or working with external legal experts can help organizations navigate the complex legal landscape and mitigate regulatory risks.

Organizations should invest in understanding the regulatory environment in all jurisdictions where they operate. This involves identifying relevant laws, regulations, and guidelines that apply to their blockchain activities. Building relationships with regulators can help organizations stay informed about regulatory changes and participate in shaping policies. Open communication with regulators can also provide clarity on compliance requirements and reduce the risk of regulatory enforcement actions.

In addition, organizations should develop and implement comprehensive compliance programs that address all relevant regulatory requirements. This includes establishing internal policies and procedures for AML/KYC compliance, data protection, securities regulation, and tax reporting. Working with legal experts who specialize in blockchain and cryptocurrency can provide valuable insights and guidance. These experts can help organizations structure their blockchain projects to comply with legal requirements and mitigate regulatory risks.

To comply with data privacy regulations, organizations can use techniques such as encryption, zero-knowledge proofs, and off-chain storage to protect personal data. These methods can help balance the need for transparency with the requirement for data privacy. Structure token offerings carefully: For organizations conducting token offerings, it is essential to determine whether the tokens are classified as securities and comply with relevant securities laws. This may involve registering the offering with regulatory authorities or structuring it to qualify for an exemption.

When using smart contracts, organizations should work with legal professionals to ensure that the contracts are enforceable and include provisions for dispute resolution. This helps address potential legal issues and ensures that the contracts operate as intended. The regulatory landscape for blockchain is continually evolving. Organizations should establish processes to monitor regulatory developments and adapt their compliance strategies accordingly. This proactive approach helps ensure ongoing compliance and reduces the risk of legal issues.

Joining industry associations and working groups focused on blockchain and cryptocurrency can provide valuable insights and advocacy opportunities. These groups can help organizations stay informed about regulatory trends and contribute to the development of favorable regulatory frameworks. Regular audits of blockchain activities can help organizations identify and address compliance issues before they become significant problems. Audits should include reviews of AML/KYC procedures, data protection practices, and tax reporting to ensure ongoing compliance with relevant regulations.

While blockchain technology offers significant benefits, it also presents substantial regulatory and legal challenges that organizations must address. By conducting thorough research, engaging with regulatory authorities, implementing robust compliance programs, leveraging legal expertise, adopting privacy-preserving techniques, carefully structuring token offerings, drafting legally sound smart contracts, monitoring regulatory developments, participating in industry groups, and conducting regular audits, organizations can navigate the complex regulatory landscape and mitigate legal risks. These strategies ensure that organizations can fully leverage the transformative potential of blockchain technology while maintaining compliance and minimizing legal exposure.

Navigating compliance issues and data privacy concerns is critical for organizations adopting blockchain technology. Ensuring compliance with existing laws and regulations is a primary challenge, as blockchain intersects with various legal domains such as finance, data protection, and contract law. For instance, financial institutions utilizing blockchain must adhere to anti-money laundering (AML) and know-your-customer (KYC) regulations, which mandate rigorous verification of participants in financial transactions. The pseudonymous nature of many blockchain platforms complicates the identification and verification process, posing significant compliance hurdles.

Data privacy is another pressing concern, particularly with regulations like the General Data Protection Regulation (GDPR) in Europe imposing strict requirements on data collection, storage, and processing. Blockchain's immutable ledger, where data cannot be easily altered or deleted, often conflicts with GDPR provisions like the right to be forgotten. Organizations must devise strategies to comply with data privacy laws while leveraging blockchain's benefits, potentially through the use of encryption techniques or off-chain storage solutions to safeguard personal information.

Securities regulation is particularly relevant for blockchain projects involving token issuance. Regulatory bodies, such as the U.S. Securities and Exchange Commission (SEC), have classified certain tokens as securities, subjecting them to rigorous regulatory standards. Initial Coin Offerings (ICOs) and Security Token Offerings (STOs) must comply with securities laws, including registration and disclosure requirements. This necessitates a clear understanding of the legal status of tokens and careful structuring of token offerings to avoid regulatory pitfalls.

Jurisdictional challenges arise because blockchain operates globally, transcending national boundaries. Different countries have varying regulatory approaches to blockchain and cryptocurrencies, creating a fragmented legal landscape.

Organizations must ensure compliance with the regulations of all jurisdictions in which they operate, a complex and resource-intensive task. The continuously evolving regulatory frameworks require organizations to stay informed about changes and adapt their strategies accordingly.

Intellectual property rights are also impacted by blockchain technology. The decentralized and open-source nature of many blockchain platforms complicates the protection and enforcement of intellectual property. Organizations need to navigate issues related to the ownership of blockchain code, patents for blockchain innovations, and the licensing of blockchain-based software. Establishing clear intellectual property policies and engaging with legal experts can help mitigate these risks.

Smart contracts present unique legal challenges, despite their potential to automate and enforce agreements. Questions about enforceability, legal recognition, and liability arise with smart contracts. For example, determining which jurisdiction's laws apply to a smart contract executed across multiple countries can be complex. Additionally, issues can occur if the smart contract code contains errors or if unforeseen circumstances affect the contract's execution. Organizations must work with legal professionals to draft smart contracts that are legally sound and include provisions for dispute resolution.

Taxation is another critical area of concern. The taxation of blockchain transactions, including cryptocurrency trading, mining rewards, and token offerings, varies significantly across jurisdictions. Organizations must understand the tax implications of their blockchain activities and ensure accurate reporting and compliance. This may involve working with tax advisors specializing in cryptocurrency and blockchain taxation.

Addressing these compliance and data privacy challenges requires developing comprehensive compliance strategies. Staying informed about relevant regulations, engaging with regulatory bodies, and participating in industry groups that advocate for favorable regulatory frameworks are essential steps. Establishing a dedicated compliance team or working with external legal experts can help navigate the complex legal landscape and mitigate regulatory risks.

Organizations should conduct thorough regulatory research to understand the regulatory environment in all jurisdictions where they operate. Building relationships with regulators can help organizations stay informed about regulatory changes and participate in shaping policies. Open communication with regulators can provide clarity on compliance requirements and reduce the risk of regulatory enforcement actions.

Implementing robust compliance programs is crucial. Organizations should develop and implement comprehensive compliance programs addressing all relevant regulatory requirements, including AML/KYC compliance, data protection, securities regulation, and tax reporting. Leveraging legal expertise by working with legal experts specializing in blockchain and cryptocurrency can provide valuable insights and guidance, helping organizations structure their blockchain projects to comply with legal requirements and mitigate regulatory risks.

Adopting privacy-preserving techniques, such as encryption, zero-knowledge proofs, and off-chain storage, can help balance the need for transparency with the requirement for data privacy. These methods protect personal data while complying with data privacy regulations.

Carefully structuring token offerings is essential for organizations conducting token offerings. Determining whether tokens are classified as securities and complying with relevant securities laws may involve registering the offering with regulatory authorities or structuring it to qualify for an exemption.

Drafting legally sound smart contracts by working with legal professionals ensures that contracts are enforceable and include provisions for dispute resolution. This addresses potential legal issues and ensures contracts operate as intended.

Monitoring regulatory developments and establishing processes to adapt compliance strategies accordingly is crucial. The regulatory landscape for blockchain is continually evolving, and a proactive approach ensures ongoing compliance and reduces the risk of legal issues.

Participating in industry groups focused on blockchain and cryptocurrency provides valuable insights and advocacy opportunities. These groups help organizations stay informed about regulatory trends and contribute to developing favorable regulatory frameworks.

Conducting regular audits of blockchain activities helps organizations identify and address compliance issues before they become significant problems. Audits should include reviews of AML/KYC procedures, data protection practices, and tax reporting to ensure ongoing compliance with relevant regulations.

Intellectual property rights in the blockchain context present unique challenges and opportunities due to the technology's decentralized and open-source nature. Protecting and enforcing intellectual property becomes more complex when traditional ownership concepts are applied to a decentralized ecosystem. Blockchain's inherent transparency can conflict with the need to keep certain intellectual properties confidential, such as proprietary algorithms or business strategies.

In the blockchain context, one of the main issues is the ownership of blockchain code. Many blockchain projects are developed as open-source software, allowing anyone to view, use, and modify the code. This open-source nature fosters innovation and collaboration but also complicates the attribution of intellectual property rights. Developers contributing to open-source projects may not have clear ownership or control over their contributions, leading to potential disputes over intellectual property.

Patents for blockchain innovations pose another significant challenge. The rapid pace of technological advancement in blockchain means that patent offices may struggle to keep up, potentially granting patents for ideas that are already common knowledge in the industry. This can lead to an increase in patent disputes and litigation, as companies vie to protect their innovations while navigating a crowded and evolving patent landscape.

Licensing blockchain-based software also requires careful consideration. Open-source licenses, such as the General Public License (GPL) or the MIT License, dictate how software can be used, modified, and distributed. Organizations must choose appropriate licenses for their projects to ensure that their intellectual property is protected while still promoting innovation and collaboration. Misunderstanding or misapplying these licenses can lead to legal complications and undermine the intended use of the software. Establishing clear intellectual property policies is crucial for organizations working with blockchain technology. These policies should define the ownership of contributions, outline the use of open-source code, and address the management of patents and licenses. By setting clear guidelines, organizations can mitigate disputes and ensure that their intellectual property is adequately protected.

Collaboration with legal experts who specialize in blockchain intellectual property can provide valuable insights and guidance. These experts can help navigate the complex landscape of blockchain IP, assist in drafting policies, and offer strategies for protecting and enforcing intellectual property rights. This collaboration ensures that organizations can innovate with confidence, knowing that their intellectual property is secure.

In addition to traditional intellectual property protections, blockchain itself can be used to enhance IP management. Blockchain's immutable ledger can provide a transparent and tamper-proof record of intellectual property ownership, creation dates, and usage rights. This can simplify the process of proving ownership and defending against infringement claims. For example, artists and content creators can use blockchain to register their works, ensuring a clear and verifiable record of authorship.

Blockchain can facilitate new business models for intellectual property, such as decentralized marketplaces for digital assets. These platforms allow creators to license their work directly to consumers, bypassing traditional intermediaries and retaining greater control over their IP. Smart contracts can automate royalty payments and usage rights, ensuring that creators are fairly compensated for their work.

Intellectual property rights in the blockchain context require careful navigation due to the technology's decentralized and open-source nature. Organizations must establish clear policies, choose appropriate licenses, and collaborate with legal experts to protect and enforce their intellectual property. Blockchain itself offers innovative solutions for IP management, providing transparent records and enabling new business models. By addressing these challenges, organizations can foster innovation while ensuring that their intellectual property remains secure.

The evolving regulatory landscape for blockchain technology presents both opportunities and challenges for organizations. As blockchain applications expand across various sectors, regulators worldwide are working to develop frameworks that address the unique aspects of this technology while protecting consumers and maintaining market integrity. This evolving landscape has significant implications for how organizations operate and innovate with blockchain.

One of the primary implications is the need for continuous compliance. As regulatory bodies introduce new laws and guidelines, organizations must stay informed and ensure that their blockchain initiatives adhere to these evolving standards. This requires a proactive approach to regulatory monitoring and the ability to quickly adapt to changes. Failure to comply with new regulations can result in legal penalties, financial losses, and reputational damage.

The decentralization inherent in blockchain technology complicates traditional regulatory approaches, which often rely on centralized control and oversight. Regulators are grappling with how to apply existing frameworks to decentralized networks and are considering new approaches tailored to the unique characteristics of blockchain. This uncertainty can create challenges for organizations trying to navigate compliance, as the rules may vary significantly between jurisdictions and can change rapidly.

Jurisdictional differences in blockchain regulation mean that organizations operating globally must navigate a complex patchwork of legal requirements. Some countries have embraced blockchain technology, implementing supportive regulatory frameworks that encourage innovation and investment. Others have imposed stringent regulations or outright bans on certain blockchain activities, such as cryptocurrency trading. Organizations must carefully assess the regulatory environments in each jurisdiction they operate in and tailor their strategies accordingly.

Data privacy regulations, such as the European Union's General Data Protection Regulation (GDPR), pose particular challenges for blockchain implementations. GDPR mandates strict controls over personal data, including the right to be forgotten, which conflicts with blockchain's immutable nature. Organizations must find ways to balance compliance with data privacy laws while leveraging blockchain's benefits. This may involve using techniques like encryption and off-chain storage to protect personal data while maintaining the integrity of the blockchain.

Regulatory clarity is crucial for fostering innovation and investment in blockchain technology. Uncertainty or overly restrictive regulations can stifle innovation and deter businesses from exploring blockchain applications. Conversely, clear and supportive regulatory frameworks can provide the confidence needed for organizations to invest in and develop new blockchain solutions. Regulators are increasingly recognizing the need to strike a balance between protecting consumers and enabling innovation.

Engagement with regulators and policymakers is essential for organizations to navigate the evolving regulatory landscape effectively. By participating in industry groups, public consultations, and regulatory sandboxes, organizations can help shape the development of regulations and ensure that their perspectives are considered. This proactive engagement can also provide insights into regulatory trends and upcoming changes, allowing organizations to prepare and adapt more effectively.

The evolving regulatory landscape also presents opportunities for organizations to demonstrate leadership and build trust. By adhering to best practices and maintaining high standards of compliance, organizations can differentiate themselves in the market and gain a competitive advantage. Transparency in operations and proactive communication about compliance efforts can enhance reputation and foster trust among customers, investors, and partners.

The evolving regulatory landscape for blockchain technology presents significant implications for organizations. Continuous compliance, proactive engagement with regulators, and the ability to adapt to changing legal environments are crucial for successfully navigating this landscape. By understanding and addressing the regulatory challenges, organizations can foster innovation, build trust, and leverage the full potential of blockchain technology.

Navigating blockchain implementation within existing legal frameworks requires a strategic and informed approach. Organizations must first thoroughly understand the relevant laws and regulations that apply to their blockchain activities. This involves continuous monitoring of legal developments across different jurisdictions, as blockchain's global nature often intersects with varying regional regulations.

A proactive approach to compliance is essential. Organizations should establish dedicated compliance teams or collaborate with external legal experts specializing in blockchain and cryptocurrency. These teams can provide guidance on structuring projects to meet regulatory requirements, such as anti-money laundering (AML) and know-your-customer (KYC) laws, which mandate detailed verification processes to prevent illicit activities.

Data privacy laws, particularly stringent in regions like the European Union with its General Data Protection Regulation (GDPR), pose specific challenges. Blockchain's immutable ledger conflicts with the GDPR's provisions for data alteration or deletion. Organizations must devise strategies, like encryption and off-chain storage, to balance the benefits of blockchain with the need for data privacy compliance.

The classification of blockchain tokens under securities law is another complex area. Tokens may be deemed securities by regulators like the U.S. Securities and Exchange Commission (SEC), subjecting them to rigorous regulations. Organizations must ensure their token offerings are structured to comply with securities regulations, including necessary registrations and disclosures, to avoid legal repercussions.

Jurisdictional challenges arise due to the decentralized and borderless nature of blockchain. Different countries have diverse regulatory approaches, from supportive frameworks to outright bans. Organizations operating globally must tailor their strategies to navigate this regulatory patchwork effectively, ensuring compliance in each jurisdiction they operate within.

Smart contracts introduce further legal considerations. These self-executing contracts, embedded with the terms of agreements, need to be legally sound. Organizations must work with legal professionals to ensure smart contracts are enforceable and include provisions for dispute resolution, addressing potential issues that could arise from coding errors or unforeseen circumstances.

Taxation of blockchain transactions, including trading, mining rewards, and token offerings, varies widely. Accurate reporting and compliance with tax regulations are crucial. Engaging with tax advisors who specialize in blockchain can help organizations navigate the complex tax landscape.

Establishing clear intellectual property policies is vital for managing blockchain innovations. Organizations must define ownership rights, use open-source code responsibly, and protect their intellectual property through patents and licenses. Legal experts can assist in drafting these policies and addressing disputes.

Participating in industry groups and engaging with regulators are proactive steps that can help shape favorable regulatory frameworks. By contributing to public consultations and regulatory sandboxes, organizations can influence policy development and gain insights into upcoming regulatory changes, allowing for better preparation and adaptation.

Navigating blockchain implementation within existing legal frameworks requires a strategic, informed, and proactive approach. Continuous legal monitoring, dedicated compliance efforts, collaboration with legal experts, and active engagement with regulators are crucial for ensuring compliance and leveraging the full potential of blockchain technology. Organizations must balance the innovative aspects of blockchain with regulatory requirements to achieve successful and legally sound implementation.

Ensuring legal and regulatory compliance when implementing blockchain technology involves adopting several best practices to navigate the complex legal landscape effectively. Organizations must conduct thorough regulatory research to understand the specific laws and guidelines that apply to their blockchain activities across different jurisdictions. This comprehensive understanding forms the foundation for compliance efforts and helps identify any potential legal challenges early on.

Engaging with regulatory authorities is crucial for maintaining open lines of communication and gaining clarity on compliance requirements. By building relationships with regulators, organizations can stay informed about regulatory changes and actively participate in shaping policies that affect their operations. This proactive engagement helps reduce the risk of regulatory enforcement actions and fosters a cooperative approach to compliance.

Developing and implementing robust compliance programs is essential. These programs should address all relevant regulatory requirements, including anti-money laundering (AML) and know-your-customer (KYC) regulations, data protection laws, securities regulations, and tax obligations. Comprehensive internal policies and procedures ensure that compliance efforts are systematic and consistent across the organization.

Leveraging legal expertise is a key strategy for navigating the regulatory landscape. Organizations should collaborate with legal experts who specialize in blockchain and cryptocurrency to gain valuable insights and guidance. These experts can assist in structuring blockchain projects to comply with legal requirements and provide advice on mitigating regulatory risks.

To comply with data privacy regulations, organizations can adopt privacy-preserving techniques such as encryption, zero-knowledge proofs, and off-chain storage. These methods help balance the need for transparency with the requirement for data protection, ensuring that personal information is safeguarded while leveraging the benefits of blockchain technology.

Carefully structuring token offerings is critical for regulatory compliance. Organizations must determine whether tokens are classified as securities and adhere to the relevant securities laws. This may involve registering the token offering with regulatory authorities or structuring it to qualify for an exemption, ensuring that all legal requirements are met.

Drafting legally sound smart contracts is another important consideration. Organizations should work with legal professionals to ensure that smart contracts are enforceable and include provisions for dispute resolution. This legal scrutiny helps address potential issues that could arise from coding errors or unforeseen circumstances, ensuring that contracts operate as intended.

Monitoring regulatory developments is essential for staying compliant in a rapidly evolving landscape. Organizations should establish processes to keep abreast of regulatory changes and adapt their compliance strategies accordingly. This proactive approach helps ensure ongoing compliance and reduces the risk of legal issues.

Participating in industry groups focused on blockchain and cryptocurrency provides valuable advocacy opportunities and insights. By joining these groups, organizations can stay informed about regulatory trends and contribute to the development of favorable regulatory frameworks, helping to shape the future of the industry.

Conducting regular audits of blockchain activities is a best practice that helps organizations identify and address compliance issues before they become significant problems. Audits should include reviews of AML/KYC procedures, data protection practices, and tax reporting to ensure that all regulatory requirements are consistently met.

Ensuring legal and regulatory compliance in blockchain implementation requires a strategic and informed approach. By conducting thorough regulatory research, engaging with authorities, developing robust compliance programs, leveraging legal expertise, adopting privacy-preserving techniques, carefully structuring token offerings, drafting legally sound smart contracts, monitoring regulatory developments, participating in industry groups, and conducting regular audits, organizations can navigate the complex legal landscape and mitigate regulatory risks effectively.

# Chapter 6: Future Outlook and Recommendations

Insights into the future of blockchain technology suggest that it will continue to evolve and significantly impact various industries. As blockchain matures, its applications will expand beyond the initial focus on cryptocurrencies and finance, penetrating deeper into sectors like healthcare, supply chain, energy, and governance. The technology's core principles—decentralization, transparency, and immutability—will drive innovations that enhance efficiency, security, and trust in digital transactions.

Interoperability will become a critical focus, as the need for different blockchain networks to communicate and operate seamlessly with each other grows. Solutions like cross-chain protocols and interoperable standards will enable disparate blockchain systems to share data and transact more efficiently, fostering a more cohesive blockchain ecosystem.

The integration of blockchain with other emerging technologies such as artificial intelligence (AI), the Internet of Things (IoT), and big data analytics will open up new possibilities. For instance, combining blockchain with AI can enhance decision-making processes, while IoT devices secured by blockchain can ensure data integrity and automate processes across smart cities and industries.

Regulatory frameworks will continue to evolve, providing clearer guidelines for blockchain adoption. Governments and regulatory bodies worldwide are recognizing the potential of blockchain and are working towards creating balanced regulations that protect consumers while encouraging innovation. This regulatory clarity will boost investor confidence and drive wider adoption of blockchain solutions.

Privacy-focused blockchain solutions will gain traction as data protection remains a top priority. Innovations in privacy-preserving technologies, such as zero-knowledge proofs and secure multi-party computation, will enable blockchain applications to comply with stringent data privacy laws without compromising transparency and security.

The adoption of Central Bank Digital Currencies (CBDCs) will also influence the future of blockchain. Several central banks are exploring or piloting CBDCs, which leverage blockchain technology to provide secure, efficient, and inclusive payment systems. The successful implementation of CBDCs could accelerate the integration of blockchain into mainstream financial systems, promoting broader acceptance and usage.

Decentralized Finance (DeFi) will continue to grow, offering alternative financial services that are more accessible and transparent than traditional banking. DeFi platforms will expand their offerings, from lending and borrowing to more complex financial instruments, attracting a wider user base and increasing the sophistication of decentralized financial ecosystems.

Environmental sustainability will become a critical concern for blockchain technology. The high energy consumption associated with certain consensus mechanisms, like Proof of Work, has raised environmental issues. Future developments will focus on more sustainable alternatives, such as Proof of Stake and other energy-efficient consensus algorithms, to reduce the environmental impact of blockchain operations. Education and talent development will play a crucial role in the future of blockchain. As demand for blockchain expertise grows, educational institutions and organizations will need to offer specialized training and certification programs to equip the workforce with the necessary skills. This emphasis on education will help bridge the talent gap and support the continued growth and innovation in the blockchain space.

Recommendations for organizations looking to leverage blockchain technology include staying informed about the latest developments and trends in the industry. Engaging with the broader blockchain community through conferences, workshops, and industry groups can provide valuable insights and foster collaboration. Organizations should also invest in research and development to explore new blockchain applications and integrate them with their existing systems.

Building strong relationships with regulators and policymakers is essential to navigate the evolving regulatory landscape. By participating in regulatory discussions and providing feedback, organizations can help shape favorable policies and ensure their compliance strategies are aligned with legal requirements. Fostering a culture of innovation and continuous learning within the organization will enable teams to experiment with blockchain solutions and adapt to new challenges and opportunities. Encouraging cross-functional collaboration and providing resources for skill development will help employees stay engaged and contribute to blockchain initiatives.

Organizations should prioritize security and privacy in their blockchain implementations. Implementing robust security measures, conducting regular audits, and adopting privacy-preserving technologies will protect sensitive data and maintain stakeholder trust. Finally, organizations should focus on sustainability by exploring energy-efficient blockchain solutions and considering the environmental impact of their blockchain activities. Adopting sustainable practices will not only reduce operational costs but also align with global efforts to address climate change.

The future of blockchain technology is promising, with continued innovation and expanding applications across various industries. By staying informed, engaging with regulators, fostering a culture of innovation, prioritizing security and privacy, and focusing on sustainability, organizations can effectively leverage blockchain technology to drive growth and create value in the evolving digital landscape.

The potential impact of blockchain technology on leadership and organizational structures is profound, necessitating significant shifts in how organizations are managed and led. Blockchain's decentralized nature challenges traditional hierarchical leadership models, promoting a more distributed approach to decision-making. This shift requires leaders to adapt by embracing collaborative and networked leadership styles, where authority and decision-making power are shared more broadly across the organization.

Leaders will need to cultivate a culture of transparency and accountability. Blockchain's transparent ledger system ensures that all actions and transactions are visible and immutable, which can help build trust both within the organization and with external stakeholders. Leaders must model transparency and encourage open communication, making information readily accessible to everyone involved.

The adoption of decentralized autonomous organizations (DAOs) is likely to increase, further disrupting traditional organizational structures. In DAOs, decision-making is conducted through token-based voting systems, where stakeholders have a direct say in the governance and strategic direction of the organization. This democratic approach requires leaders to facilitate consensus-building processes and manage diverse stakeholder interests effectively. As blockchain technology integrates with other emerging technologies such as artificial intelligence (AI) and the Internet of Things (IoT), leaders will need to be adept at managing interdisciplinary teams and fostering innovation. This integration will demand a higher degree of flexibility and a willingness to experiment with new business models and operational processes.

Organizational structures will become more fluid and adaptable. Traditional boundaries between departments and functions may blur as blockchain enables more seamless collaboration across the organization. This interconnectedness will require leaders to focus on building strong internal networks and fostering a culture of collaboration and continuous learning.

Blockchain technology will also impact governance practices. Traditional governance models, which often rely on centralized oversight, will need to evolve to accommodate the decentralized nature of blockchain. Organizations might adopt new governance frameworks that distribute decision-making power more evenly and incorporate stakeholder input more directly. This shift will require leaders to develop new skills in facilitation and conflict resolution to manage the complexities of decentralized governance.

Trust and security will be paramount in the blockchain era. Leaders must ensure that robust security measures are in place to protect the integrity of the blockchain and the data it contains. This involves regular security audits, the implementation of advanced cryptographic techniques, and ongoing education and training for employees on best security practices.

The talent landscape will also change significantly. As blockchain technology becomes more prevalent, there will be an increasing demand for skilled professionals who understand blockchain development, smart contracts, and related technologies. Leaders will need to invest in talent development, offering training and certification programs to build the necessary skills within their workforce.

Leaders must navigate the ethical implications of blockchain technology. Issues such as data privacy, consent, and the potential for misuse of blockchain must be carefully managed. Establishing clear ethical guidelines and ensuring compliance with regulatory standards will be crucial for maintaining the organization's integrity and reputation.

The integration of blockchain will also drive efficiency gains and process improvements. Smart contracts and automated workflows will streamline operations, reducing the need for intermediaries and minimizing human error. Leaders will need to oversee the transition to these new processes, ensuring that employees are supported and that the benefits of automation are fully realized.

Blockchain technology will significantly impact leadership and organizational structures, driving shifts towards more decentralized, transparent, and collaborative models. Leaders will need to adapt by fostering a culture of openness, embracing new governance frameworks, investing in talent development, and ensuring robust security and ethical practices. By doing so, they can effectively navigate the complexities of blockchain adoption and harness its potential to drive organizational success and innovation.

To effectively embrace blockchain technology, leaders must first educate themselves and their teams about its fundamentals and potential applications. Understanding blockchain's core principles and how it can be integrated into existing systems is crucial for informed decision-making. Leaders should engage with industry experts, attend relevant conferences, and participate in blockchain-focused forums to stay updated on the latest developments.

Building a strategic vision for blockchain adoption is essential. Leaders need to identify specific areas within their organization where blockchain can add value, such as enhancing transparency, improving security, or streamlining processes. This strategic vision should be aligned with the organization's overall goals and objectives, ensuring that blockchain initiatives support broader business strategies.

Fostering a culture of innovation and experimentation is vital. Leaders should encourage their teams to explore blockchain applications and pilot projects that can demonstrate the technology's benefits. This involves creating a supportive environment where experimentation is welcomed, and failures are seen as learning opportunities. Providing resources and time for these explorations can drive creativity and innovation.

Collaboration across departments is necessary to break down silos and ensure a cohesive approach to blockchain implementation. Leaders should promote cross-functional teams that bring together diverse expertise, including IT, legal, compliance, and business units. These teams can work collaboratively to develop and implement blockchain solutions that address the organization's unique challenges and opportunities.

Investing in training and development is critical to build the necessary skills within the organization. Leaders should provide opportunities for employees to learn about blockchain technology through workshops, courses, and certification programs. This investment in human capital ensures that the organization has the expertise needed to successfully implement and manage blockchain initiatives.

Establishing strong partnerships with external blockchain experts and technology providers can enhance the organization's capabilities. Leaders should seek out collaborations with blockchain developers, consultants, and industry groups to gain insights and access to cutting-edge solutions. These partnerships can accelerate the implementation process and provide valuable support.

Ensuring robust security measures is paramount when adopting blockchain technology. Leaders must prioritize cybersecurity by implementing advanced cryptographic techniques, conducting regular security audits, and staying vigilant against potential threats. Protecting the integrity of the blockchain and the data it contains is essential for maintaining trust and operational stability.

Proactive engagement with regulators and policymakers is necessary to navigate the evolving regulatory landscape. Leaders should build relationships with regulatory bodies, participate in public consultations, and advocate for favorable policies. Understanding and complying with regulatory requirements helps mitigate legal risks and ensures that blockchain initiatives are sustainable and legally sound.

Transparent communication about blockchain initiatives is crucial for gaining stakeholder buy-in. Leaders should clearly articulate the benefits and objectives of blockchain projects to employees, investors, customers, and partners. Regular updates and open discussions about progress and challenges help build trust and foster a supportive environment for blockchain adoption.

Leaders must also address the ethical considerations of blockchain technology. Establishing clear guidelines on data privacy, consent, and responsible use is essential. Ensuring that blockchain applications comply with ethical standards and regulatory requirements protects the organization's reputation and builds stakeholder trust.

Continuously monitoring and evaluating blockchain projects helps ensure they deliver the intended benefits. Leaders should establish metrics to assess the performance of blockchain initiatives and make data-driven decisions to refine and improve them. Regular reviews and adjustments ensure that blockchain implementations remain aligned with organizational goals and adapt to changing conditions.

Leaders can effectively embrace blockchain technology by educating themselves and their teams, building a strategic vision, fostering a culture of innovation, promoting cross-functional collaboration, investing in training, establishing strong partnerships, ensuring robust security, engaging with regulators, communicating transparently, addressing ethical considerations, and continuously monitoring progress. By adopting these practices, leaders can harness the transformative potential of blockchain to drive organizational success and innovation. Fostering innovation and staying ahead of the curve with blockchain technology requires a proactive and strategic approach. Leaders must create an environment that encourages exploration and experimentation with new ideas. This involves not only supporting pilot projects but also providing the necessary resources and autonomy for teams to innovate without fear of failure. Embracing a mindset that views setbacks as learning opportunities is essential for driving continuous improvement and breakthrough innovations.

Investing in research and development is critical. Organizations should allocate budget and resources to explore emerging blockchain technologies and their potential applications. Collaborating with academic institutions, industry consortia, and research organizations can provide valuable insights and accelerate innovation. Keeping abreast of the latest trends and technological advancements through these partnerships ensures that the organization remains at the forefront of blockchain development.

Developing a culture of continuous learning within the organization is vital. Leaders should encourage employees to stay informed about the latest blockchain developments by participating in workshops, webinars, and conferences. Providing access to educational resources and fostering a learning environment helps build a knowledgeable and skilled workforce capable of driving innovation. Encouraging cross-functional collaboration enhances the innovation process by bringing together diverse perspectives and expertise. Leaders should facilitate opportunities for teams from different departments to work together on blockchain projects. This collaborative approach fosters creative problem-solving and leads to more holistic and effective solutions.

Leveraging external expertise and establishing partnerships with blockchain innovators can provide a competitive edge. Engaging with blockchain startups, technology providers, and consultants allows organizations to access cutting-edge solutions and industry best practices. These collaborations can also provide fresh insights and new approaches to leveraging blockchain technology.

Staying agile and adaptable is crucial in the rapidly evolving blockchain landscape. Leaders must be willing to pivot strategies and adapt to new information and changing market conditions. This requires a flexible organizational structure and decision-making processes that allow for quick adjustments and responsiveness to emerging opportunities.

Maintaining a strong focus on customer needs and market demands ensures that blockchain innovations are relevant and valuable. Leaders should actively seek feedback from customers and stakeholders to inform the development of blockchain solutions. Understanding market trends and anticipating future demands helps organizations stay ahead of the curve and deliver products and services that meet evolving expectations.

Proactively addressing regulatory challenges and engaging with policymakers is essential for creating a favorable environment for blockchain innovation. Leaders should participate in industry discussions and advocacy efforts to shape regulatory frameworks that support blockchain development. Staying informed about regulatory changes and ensuring compliance helps mitigate risks and positions the organization as a responsible and forward-thinking leader in the blockchain space.

Incorporating ethical considerations into the innovation process is crucial for building trust and sustainability. Leaders must ensure that blockchain applications adhere to ethical standards and promote transparency, data privacy, and responsible use. By prioritizing ethical practices, organizations can enhance their reputation and build long-term trust with stakeholders.

Continuous evaluation and refinement of blockchain initiatives are necessary to ensure ongoing relevance and effectiveness. Leaders should establish metrics to measure the impact of blockchain projects and use this data to make informed decisions about improvements and future developments. Regularly assessing the performance of blockchain solutions helps identify areas for optimization and drives sustained innovation By fostering a culture of innovation, investing in research and development, encouraging collaboration, leveraging external expertise, staying agile, focusing on customer needs, addressing regulatory challenges, incorporating ethical considerations, and continuously evaluating initiatives, leaders can ensure their organizations remain at the forefront of blockchain technology. This strategic approach enables organizations to harness the transformative potential of blockchain and maintain a competitive advantage in a rapidly changing digital landscape.

Preparing organizations for a blockchain-enabled future involves creating a strategic vision that aligns with the organization's goals and objectives. This vision should identify areas where blockchain can drive innovation, enhance efficiency, and improve transparency. Leaders must educate themselves and their teams about blockchain technology, ensuring a deep understanding of its principles, benefits, and potential applications.

Investing in talent development is crucial. Organizations should provide training programs and resources to help employees build the necessary skills to work with blockchain. Encouraging continuous learning and staying updated on industry trends ensures the workforce is prepared to leverage new opportunities as they arise.

Nurturing a culture of innovation is essential. Leaders should create an environment that encourages experimentation and accepts failure as part of the learning process. This involves supporting pilot projects and allowing teams the freedom to explore blockchain applications that could transform business processes.

Establishing strong governance frameworks is vital for managing blockchain initiatives. This includes setting clear policies and guidelines to ensure compliance with regulatory requirements and ethical standards. Regularly reviewing and updating these frameworks helps maintain alignment with evolving laws and industry best practices. Enhancing cybersecurity measures is paramount in a blockchain-enabled environment. Organizations must implement robust security protocols to protect blockchain networks and data from potential threats. Regular security audits and adopting advanced cryptographic techniques can safeguard the integrity of blockchain systems.

Building cross-functional teams promotes collaboration and integrates diverse perspectives in blockchain projects. Leaders should facilitate cooperation between departments, such as IT, legal, finance, and operations, to ensure a holistic approach to blockchain implementation. This collaboration can lead to more innovative and effective solutions.

Engaging with external partners, such as blockchain experts, technology providers, and industry consortia, can provide valuable insights and accelerate blockchain adoption. These partnerships enable organizations to access cutting-edge technology, share knowledge, and collaborate on developing industry standards.

Maintaining agility and adaptability allows organizations to respond quickly to changes in the blockchain landscape. This involves being open to adjusting strategies and processes as new information and technologies emerge. A flexible approach ensures that organizations can capitalize on emerging opportunities and stay ahead of competitors. Focusing on customer needs and market trends helps organizations develop blockchain solutions that deliver real value. Leaders should actively seek feedback from customers and stakeholders to inform blockchain initiatives. Understanding market demands and anticipating future trends positions the organization to meet evolving expectations effectively.

Proactively addressing regulatory challenges is essential for ensuring compliance and fostering a supportive environment for blockchain innovation. Organizations should stay informed about regulatory developments, engage with policymakers, and participate in industry advocacy efforts to shape favorable regulations. This proactive approach helps mitigate legal risks and supports sustainable growth.

Incorporating ethical considerations into blockchain projects builds trust and enhances the organization's reputation. Leaders must ensure that blockchain applications adhere to ethical standards, promote data privacy, and encourage transparency. Prioritizing ethical practices fosters long-term relationships with customers and stakeholders.

Continuous evaluation and improvement of blockchain initiatives are necessary to maintain their relevance and effectiveness. Organizations should establish metrics to assess the impact of blockchain projects and use this data to refine and optimize their strategies. Regular reviews ensure that blockchain implementations remain aligned with organizational goals and adapt to changing conditions.

By creating a strategic vision, investing in talent development, fostering a culture of innovation, establishing strong governance, enhancing cybersecurity, building cross-functional teams, engaging with external partners, maintaining agility, focusing on customer needs, addressing regulatory challenges, incorporating ethical considerations, and continuously evaluating initiatives, organizations can prepare effectively for a blockchain-enabled future. This comprehensive approach ensures that organizations can harness the transformative potential of blockchain technology and achieve sustained success in the digital age.

# Conclusion

In this book, we have explored the transformative potential of blockchain technology and its profound impact on various aspects of organizational leadership and management. We began by understanding the fundamentals of blockchain, including its principles of decentralization, transparency, and immutability, and how these principles differentiate it from traditional centralized systems. We examined the transformative potential of blockchain across multiple sectors such as finance, supply chain management, healthcare, and governance. By enabling secure, transparent, and decentralized transactions, blockchain has the capacity to revolutionize these industries, streamline processes, reduce costs, and enhance trust and transparency.

Leadership challenges and opportunities in the blockchain era were discussed, emphasizing the need for evolving traditional leadership models to embrace decentralized decision-making, distributed authority, and increased transparency. We highlighted the concept of "leadership on a blockchain," promoting networked, collaborative, and adaptive leadership styles that align with blockchain's decentralized nature.

Organizational transformation was explored, detailing the implications of adopting blockchain technology. We delved into the necessity for cultural shifts and new governance models, stressing the importance of fostering a culture of transparency, collaboration, and continuous learning. Strategies for integrating blockchain into existing systems and processes were outlined, emphasizing the importance of interoperability, data migration, and security.

We addressed the regulatory and legal considerations critical for blockchain adoption, outlining the challenges posed by the evolving regulatory landscape and the need for compliance with existing laws. Best practices for ensuring legal and regulatory compliance were provided, focusing on proactive engagement with regulators, robust compliance programs, and leveraging legal expertise.

The future outlook of blockchain technology was discussed, highlighting its expanding applications, the importance of interoperability, and the integration with other emerging technologies. We explored the potential impact on leadership and organizational structures, emphasizing the need for adaptable, transparent, and collaborative governance models.

Recommendations for leaders to embrace blockchain technology included staying informed, fostering a culture of innovation, investing in talent development, establishing strong partnerships, ensuring robust security measures, engaging with regulators, and addressing ethical considerations. We also discussed strategies for fostering innovation and staying ahead of the curve, emphasizing continuous learning, cross-functional collaboration, and customer-centric approaches.

In preparing organizations for a blockchain-enabled future, we outlined the importance of creating a strategic vision, building a knowledgeable workforce, fostering innovation, establishing strong governance frameworks, enhancing cybersecurity, and maintaining agility and adaptability.

It is evident that blockchain technology holds immense potential to transform organizational practices and drive significant advancements across various sectors. Leaders who embrace this technology and strategically integrate it into their operations will be well-positioned to navigate the challenges and capitalize on the opportunities presented by the blockchain revolution. By fostering a culture of innovation, transparency, and collaboration, organizations can harness the full potential of blockchain to achieve sustained success and drive future growth.

Leadership in the blockchain era is of paramount importance as it guides organizations through the complexities and transformative potential of this revolutionary technology. The decentralized, transparent, and immutable nature of blockchain demands a shift from traditional hierarchical leadership models to more adaptive, networked, and collaborative approaches. Leaders must cultivate an environment that embraces these principles, fostering a culture of innovation, transparency, and continuous learning.

Effective leadership is crucial for navigating the regulatory landscape, ensuring compliance with evolving laws, and engaging with policymakers to shape favorable regulatory frameworks. Leaders need to be proactive in understanding and addressing the legal challenges associated with blockchain, leveraging their knowledge to protect the organization from potential legal risks while advocating for clear and supportive regulations.

The ability to drive organizational transformation is a key attribute of leaders in the blockchain era. This involves rethinking and restructuring traditional business processes to leverage blockchain's benefits, such as enhancing transparency, improving efficiency, and reducing costs. Leaders must also build strong cross-functional teams, encouraging collaboration across departments to develop and implement innovative blockchain solutions.

Building trust both within the organization and with external stakeholders is another critical aspect of leadership in the blockchain context. Transparency and accountability, core tenets of blockchain, must be reflected in leadership practices. Leaders should model these values, ensuring that all actions and decisions are visible and justifiable, thereby fostering a culture of trust and integrity.

Leaders must also be adept at managing change and fostering a culture that embraces new technologies and methodologies. This involves investing in talent development, providing training and resources to build blockchain expertise within the organization, and creating an environment where experimentation and learning are encouraged. Strategic vision and foresight are essential for leaders to identify and capitalize on opportunities presented by blockchain technology. This includes staying informed about the latest developments and trends in the industry, understanding the potential applications of blockchain, and integrating it strategically into the organization's operations to drive growth and innovation.

The role of leadership in the blockchain era cannot be overstated. Effective leaders will be those who can navigate regulatory complexities, drive organizational transformation, build trust, manage change, and strategically integrate blockchain technology to harness its full potential. By fostering a culture of innovation, transparency, and collaboration, leaders can ensure that their organizations are well-positioned to thrive in the blockchain-enabled future.

Organizational adaptation in the blockchain era is essential for harnessing the transformative potential of this technology. Blockchain's decentralized, transparent, and immutable characteristics require organizations to rethink and restructure traditional business processes. This transformation demands agility and a willingness to embrace change at every level of the organization. Organizations must cultivate a culture that supports innovation and continuous learning. Encouraging employees to explore and experiment with blockchain applications can lead to groundbreaking solutions and improvements. Providing resources and training programs ensures that the workforce is equipped with the necessary skills and knowledge to leverage blockchain technology effectively.

Interdepartmental collaboration is vital for successful blockchain implementation. Breaking down silos and fostering teamwork across various functions allows for a more holistic approach to problem-solving and innovation. Cross-functional teams can bring diverse perspectives and expertise, leading to more effective and comprehensive blockchain solutions.

Adaptation also involves investing in robust governance frameworks that align with blockchain's decentralized nature. Traditional hierarchical structures may need to be modified to support more distributed decision-making processes. This shift requires clear policies and guidelines to ensure that decentralized operations remain efficient and compliant with regulatory standards.

Organizations must proactively engage with regulatory bodies and stay informed about evolving laws and guidelines. By participating in industry discussions and advocacy efforts, organizations can help shape regulatory frameworks that support blockchain innovation while ensuring compliance and mitigating legal risks.

Security and privacy are paramount concerns in the blockchain era. Organizations need to implement advanced cybersecurity measures and regularly conduct security audits to protect blockchain networks from potential threats. Ensuring data privacy while maintaining transparency requires careful planning and the adoption of privacy-preserving techniques.

Staying customer-centric is crucial for maintaining relevance and competitiveness. Organizations should actively seek feedback from customers and stakeholders to understand their needs and expectations. This insight can drive the development of blockchain solutions that deliver real value and enhance customer satisfaction. Continuous evaluation and improvement of blockchain initiatives are necessary to ensure they remain aligned with organizational goals and respond to changing conditions. Establishing metrics to measure the impact and effectiveness of blockchain projects allows organizations to make data-driven decisions and refine their strategies accordingly.

Organizational adaptation is crucial in the blockchain era. By fostering a culture of innovation, encouraging cross-functional collaboration, investing in governance and security, engaging with regulators, and maintaining a customer-centric approach, organizations can effectively navigate the complexities of blockchain technology. This adaptability will enable them to harness the full potential of blockchain, drive growth, and achieve sustained success in the evolving digital landscape.

Blockchain technology is an ever-evolving landscape that promises to reshape numerous industries and redefine traditional business models. As the technology matures, its applications continue to expand, moving beyond cryptocurrencies to influence sectors such as finance, supply chain management, healthcare, and governance. This evolution is driven by blockchain's core principles of decentralization, transparency, and immutability, which offer compelling advantages over conventional systems.

One of the most significant aspects of blockchain's evolution is its increasing interoperability. The development of cross-chain protocols and standards is enabling disparate blockchain networks to communicate and transact seamlessly. This advancement fosters a more integrated ecosystem where the full potential of blockchain can be realized, enhancing efficiency and enabling new use cases.

The integration of blockchain with other emerging technologies, such as artificial intelligence, the Internet of Things, and big data analytics, is opening up new possibilities for innovation. These combinations are creating powerful synergies that can transform business processes, enhance decision-making, and improve the management of complex systems.

As regulatory frameworks around the world continue to develop, greater clarity and guidance are being provided for blockchain adoption. This regulatory evolution is crucial for building trust and fostering widespread adoption. Clear and supportive regulations will encourage investment and innovation, allowing blockchain technology to thrive in a compliant and secure environment.

Privacy and security will remain at the forefront of blockchain's ongoing development. Innovations in privacy-preserving technologies, such as zero-knowledge proofs and secure multi-party computation, are addressing concerns around data privacy and security. These advancements are essential for ensuring that blockchain can be used responsibly and ethically, particularly in industries handling sensitive information.

The rise of Central Bank Digital Currencies (CBDCs) represents a significant milestone in blockchain's evolution. CBDCs have the potential to revolutionize the financial system by providing secure, efficient, and inclusive payment methods. Their successful implementation could accelerate the integration of blockchain into mainstream financial services, promoting broader acceptance and usage. Decentralized Finance (DeFi) continues to grow, offering innovative financial services that are more accessible and transparent than traditional banking. As DeFi platforms expand their offerings, they will attract a wider user base, further decentralizing financial power and democratizing access to financial services.

Sustainability is becoming a critical focus in the blockchain space. The environmental impact of blockchain operations, particularly those using energy-intensive consensus mechanisms, is driving the development of more sustainable alternatives. Adopting energy-efficient consensus algorithms and sustainable practices will be crucial for the technology's long-term viability.

Education and talent development will play a pivotal role in supporting blockchain's ongoing evolution. As the demand for blockchain expertise grows, educational institutions and organizations must offer specialized training and certification programs. Developing a skilled workforce is essential for driving innovation and ensuring that blockchain technology can reach its full potential.

The ongoing evolution of blockchain technology is marked by rapid advancements and expanding applications. As interoperability improves, regulatory frameworks develop, and privacy and security concerns are addressed, blockchain will continue to transform industries and drive innovation. Leaders and organizations that stay informed, invest in talent development, and embrace a culture of innovation will be well-positioned to leverage the transformative power of blockchain, shaping the future of the digital economy.

The implications of blockchain for the future are profound and wide-reaching, poised to transform numerous aspects of our daily lives and business operations. Blockchain's decentralized and transparent nature offers a foundation for building systems that are more secure, efficient, and trustworthy. As technology continues to evolve, its potential applications are expected to expand, leading to significant advancements across various sectors.

In finance, blockchain is set to revolutionize how transactions are conducted, reducing the need for intermediaries and lowering transaction costs. The rise of decentralized finance (DeFi) platforms will democratize access to financial services, making them more accessible to people worldwide. Additionally, the development of Central Bank Digital Currencies (CBDCs) will enhance the efficiency and security of national payment systems, potentially transforming how we use and think about money.

Supply chain management will benefit greatly from blockchain's ability to provide real-time tracking and verification of goods. This transparency can reduce fraud, improve efficiency, and ensure ethical sourcing and sustainability practices. Consumers will be able to verify the origin and journey of the products they purchase, fostering greater trust in the supply chain.

Healthcare will see improvements in data security and patient care through the adoption of blockchain. Secure and immutable patient records can enhance data sharing among healthcare providers, leading to better diagnosis and treatment outcomes. Blockchain can also ensure the authenticity of pharmaceuticals, combating counterfeit drugs and improving patient safety.

Governance and public administration stand to gain from blockchain's potential to increase transparency and accountability. Voting systems, public records, and government transactions recorded on a blockchain can reduce corruption and increase public trust in government institutions. Decentralized Autonomous Organizations (DAOs) may emerge as new models for collaborative and democratic decision-making, enabling more inclusive and participatory governance.

In intellectual property management, blockchain can provide a transparent and tamper-proof record of ownership, protecting the rights of creators and innovators. This capability can enhance the protection and monetization of digital assets, fostering a more robust and fair intellectual property ecosystem.

The future of blockchain also includes significant advancements in privacy and security technologies. As innovations like zero-knowledge proofs and secure multi-party computation become more prevalent, blockchain will offer even stronger protections for sensitive data, addressing one of the major concerns of digital transactions.

As we conclude this exploration of blockchain technology and its transformative potential, it's clear that we stand on the brink of a new era. Blockchain is not just a technological innovation; it's a paradigm shift that promises to redefine how we interact with the digital world. The implications are vast, touching every industry and aspect of society.

For leaders, innovators, and visionaries, this presents an incredible opportunity. The path forward is one of continuous learning, adaptation, and bold experimentation. Embrace the principles of decentralization, transparency, and immutability that blockchain embodies. Foster a culture within your organization that values innovation, collaboration, and ethical practices. Stay informed about the latest developments and be ready to pivot as new opportunities and challenges arise.

Remember, the journey of integrating blockchain into your business or personal endeavors is one of pioneering spirit. There will be obstacles and uncertainties, but with resilience and a forward-thinking mindset, the potential rewards are immense. You have the power to shape the future, leveraging blockchain to create systems that are more secure, efficient, and fair.

Let this exploration serve as a call to action. Dive into the blockchain world with curiosity and determination. Collaborate with others, share knowledge, and build networks that can drive collective progress. By embracing blockchain technology, you are not only positioning yourself at the forefront of innovation but also contributing to a more transparent, accountable, and equitable digital future.

As you move forward, let the principles and insights discussed in this book guide you. Be a leader who champions innovation and inspires others to see the transformative power of blockchain. Together, we can unlock new possibilities and pave the way for a future where technology serves the greater good, fostering prosperity and trust in a digital age.

Your journey with blockchain starts now. Embrace it, lead with vision, and make a lasting impact.

www.ingramcontent.com/pod-product-compliance
Lightning Source LLC
Chambersburg PA
CBHW070303230526
45470CB00002B/702